ML
917.4985 W71
Wilt, Dirk Vander
Atlantic City : beyond gambling

due 7/8

Atlantic City

Atlantic City
Beyond Gambling

Dirk Vander Wilt

Atlantic City: Beyond Gambling
Text © 2005 by Dirk Vander Wilt
Photos and maps © 2005 by Dirk Vander Wilt

Published by Parkscape Press
an imprint of Channel Lake, Inc.

New York, NY
Published in May, 2005
Version 1.0.0

All rights reserved. No part of this book may be reproduced or transmitted in any form or by any means, electronic or mechanical, including photocopying, recording, or by any information storage and retrieval system, without permission in writing from the copyright owner.

ISBN: 0-9767064-0-7
Library of Congress Control Number: 2005902408

Parkscape Press is a trademark of Channel Lake, Inc.

This book was published in the United States of America.

For more information, visit: http://www.parkscapepress.com

FOND DU LAC PUBLIC LIBRARY

ACKNOWLEDGMENTS

No book is possible to create without the help of others. I am indebted to the following:

Thanks to my editors David Pabian and Emily Wang. Thanks also to Caroline Rinaldy for additional editing and creative input.

Thanks to the Atlantic City Convention and Visitors Authority for their seemingly endless supply of information and friendly representatives.

For their tolerance while I gabbed on and on about Atlantic City, and worked on this book when I should have been doing my job, I thank my fellow staff mates at New York University.

Finally, thanks to my mother and father for their moral support.

*** IMPORTANT NOTICE ***

This book is an unauthorized review and critique of some of the many places to go and things to do in Atlantic City, New Jersey. It has not been endorsed nor approved by any of the attractions or companies listed.

An honest attempt was made to ensure accuracy of phone numbers, prices, and other information. However, neither the author nor the publisher guarantees the accuracy of anything contained herein. We therefore recommend that you use additional information sources, and contact the establishments directly for the most accurate or up-to-date information.

This book contains only the opinions of the author, and nothing should be mistaken as fact. Neither the author nor the publisher is responsible for any of the information contained in this book. Use it at *your own risk.*

One is greatly impressed with the vast numbers of resorts on the Atlantic coast. All along the Jersey shore from Bar Harbor to Cape May you will find it almost as thickly settled as a town. Here along this coast an amazing degree of congestion exists. You will marvel to see all along the beach from Sandy Hook, fifty miles of crowded street, of hotels, and houses, and behind these still others. How this vast seaside population thrills one, bringing visions of the "vastness and wealth of teeming millions" of this great nation of ours. One author says, and with truth, that Atlantic City could accommodate all of France and still have room for more while Asbury Park would furnish ample room as a seaside resort for Belgium and Holland.

Atlantic City, known throughout the world as a great all-the-year resort, is situated upon Absecon Island off the Jersey coast... Its close proximity to the large eastern centers of population give it an unrivaled location. The climate is made equable by the Gulf Stream. It is much warmer here in winter than at New York or Philadelphia and weather records show sixty-two per cent sunshine. Motorists visit the seashore metropolis by tens of thousands in all seasons of the year.

Atlantic City has one thousand two hundred hotels and boarding houses to meet every purse and entertains twenty million people annually, the transient population reaching four hundred thousand in August and never being less than fifty thousand. For six miles along one of the finest bathing beaches on the Atlantic seaboard extends the world-famed board walk, sixty feet wide, topped with planking and built upon a steel and concrete foundation, where promenade health and recreation seekers from all parts of America and foreign climes. There are four great piers varying in length from one thousand to three thousand feet, with auditoriums and all kinds of amusements which are as varied as the visitors are versatile. The shops of the board walk are one of its most attractive features.

What a motley crowd of human beings throng the board walk! How like the vast interminable deep is this thronging, surging mass of humanity, where they, like restless waves, pause awhile on the margin of the boundless sea until the ebb tide moves out in the vast sea of life. "Here the fury of fashion ebbs and flows, a constant stream, representing all the states of the Union." Here are men with silk plug hats and petite mustachios who seem "straight from Paris!" Others whose ruddy faces and commanding air proclaim them genial sons of the Emerald Isle, while still others are the possessors of so many and varied characteristics one might be justified in calling them mongrels. One would think the lovely Pleiades themselves came every night on a long journey to look at the board walk with an interrogation mark in every twinkle. Here come youth and beauty seeking pleasure. Here, too, you will see old age trying to recall their youthful days "when the serious looking canes they so carefully carry gave place to the foppish switches they so artfully carried in their younger days." Here the gilded doors of idleness and pleasure are ever ajar but they never lead to the halls of noble aims and the palaces of worthy ambition. Here the entrances are always crowded with that class of people whose motto is, "Things are good enough as they are," or "Eat, drink and be merry," or "We are weary of well doing."

Here beauty assembles, but it is ofttimes not the beauty of life. It is the glaring show and tinsel array of society that attracts great numbers, who, like the beautiful colored night moths, are enamoured of the gleaming light, venturing nearer until they scorch their wings, or blinded by the brilliant rays plunge headlong into the flames and are burned to death. "The allied army of fashion meets here." Here, then, is their Thermopylae or Argonne, it may be.

It is surprising to see that by far the greater numbers of people turn their backs on the ocean while they scan the daily papers for sensational items or the latest styles. It seems a cruel waste of glorious linden trees to say nothing of the wealth of sweets that the bees have lost to record at least some vamp's trial in a murder case or some miserably rich woman's divorce scandal. There are those who go to Europe who bring back to their native land only the latest fashions of Paris with a little knowledge of foreign profanity picked up from the cafes and boulevards. They can tell nothing about the wonders of the Louvre; the grandeur of Raphael's Madonnas; the beauty and charm of the Mediterranean shores. Their souls perhaps have never been touched by the grand sublimity of the Alps. What feasts they have attended, taking away only the husks!

Only the more hardy remain to enjoy the grandeur of the winter ocean like the chickadees and cardinal grosbeaks that enliven our winter woods. The many flowered asters remain regal and cheery though a thousands winds may blow. Those who see the real beauty and indescribable grandeur of the ocean here, if they cannot remain, will show evidences in their beneficent lives that they have had a wonderful summer by the sea. Here amid the most beautiful manifestations of Nature's power and grandeur they have gained broader hopes, higher aspirations and a purer life. They leave the frivolous things of life on its remotest shores, where a few returning tides bury them in the sands of forgetfulness or the receding waves wash them like clams far out to sea.

Excerpted from Orville O. Hiestand's See America First. Regan Printing House, Chicago. **Published in 1922.**

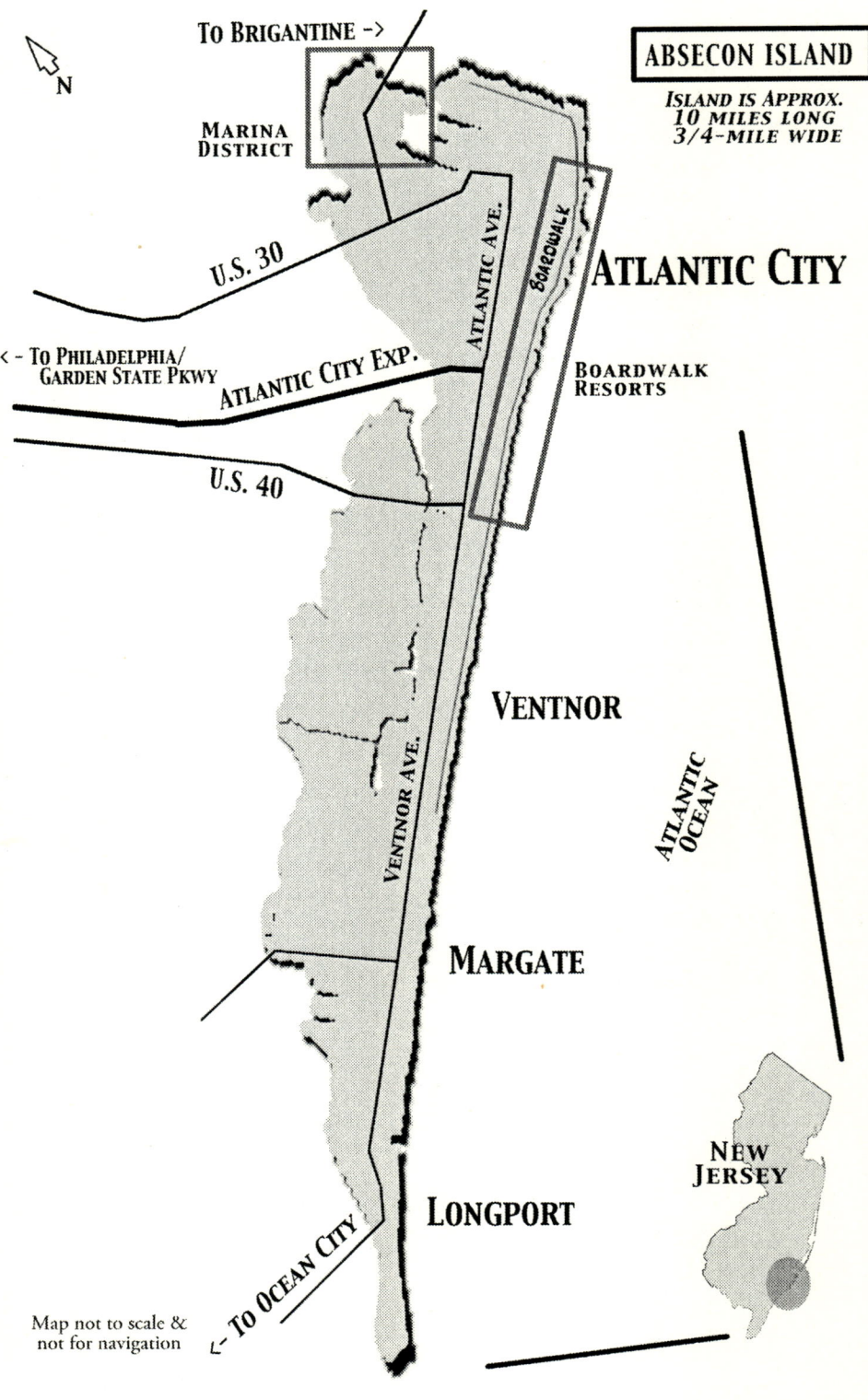

TABLE OF CONTENTS

INTRODUCTION	15
WHY VISIT ATLANTIC CITY?	21
THE ATLANTIC CITY RESORTS	43
THE BOARDWALK RESORTS	47
ATLANTIC CITY HILTON	51
TROPICANA CASINO & RESORT	55
TRUMP PLAZA	61
CAESARS ATLANTIC CITY	67
BALLY'S ATLANTIC CITY	75
BALLY'S WILD WILD WEST CASINO	76
BALLY'S PARK PLACE	80
THE CLARIDGE	86
SANDS HOTEL & CASINO	93
RESORTS ATLANTIC CITY	97
TRUMP TAJ MAHAL	101
SHOWBOAT ATLANTIC CITY	107
THE MARINA DISTRICT RESORTS	111
HARRAH'S ATLANTIC CITY	113
BORGATA HOTEL CASINO & SPA	117
TRUMP MARINA	125

AMUSEMENT CENTERS   131

STEEL PIER	131
BOARDWALK AMUSEMENTS	133
ATLANTIC CITY MINIATURE GOLF	134
PASSPORT: VOYAGES OF DISCOVERY	135
STORYBOOK LAND	137

ENTERTAINMENT AND SPORTS   139

BOARDWALK HALL	139
THE MISS AMERICA ORGANIZATION	141
KENNEDY PLAZA	142
SKATE ZONE	143
SANDCASTLE BASEBALL STADIUM	143
GOLF COURSES	144

MUSEUMS AND CULTURE   147

THE NEW JERSEY KOREAN WAR MEMORIAL	149
CIVIL RIGHTS GARDEN	149
RIPLEY'S *BELIEVE IT OR NOT!* MUSEUM	150
DR. JONATHON PITNEY HOUSE	151
ABSECON LIGHTHOUSE	152
LUCY THE ELEPHANT	153
OCEAN LIFE CENTER	156
BALIC WINERY	157
RENAULT WINERY	157
THE NOYES MUSEUM	159

PARKS AND RECREATION   161

EDWIN B. FORSYTHE NATIONAL WILDLIFE REFUGE	161
WHARTON STATE FOREST AND BATSTO VILLAGE	162
BEL HAVEN CANOES AND KAYAKS	164

HISTORIC GARDNER'S BASIN	165
BOAT CRUISES AND CHARTERS	166
EXTREME WINDSURFING	167
MARINE MAMMAL STRANDING CENTER	168

SHOPPING 169

ATLANTIC CITY OUTLETS	169
SIGANOS PLAZA	170
DOWNTOWN ATLANTIC CITY	171
FRALINGER'S SALT WATER TAFFY	172
SHORE MALL	173
HISTORIC SMITHVILLE	173
HAMILTON MALL	175

CLUBS AND NIGHTLIFE 177

CASINOS	178
CLUB TRU	178
STRIP CLUBS	179
OTHER NIGHTLIFE	181

RESOURCES 183

SELECT ACCOMMODATIONS	189
SELECT RESTAURANTS	197
TRAVEL SCENARIOS	203
INTERNET DIRECTORY	211
MORE INFORMATION	221
INDEX	223

Introduction

On the east coast, mid-way down the Jersey Shore, is the most famous gambling destination outside of Las Vegas. With over a dozen high rise casino-resorts stretching two miles down the country's first Oceanside boardwalk, it attracts thousands of people every day, and over 31 million people each year. The Parker Brothers' classic game Monopoly was influenced by its street names, and the annual Miss America pageant is held here and broadcast live from coast to coast. Like Las Vegas, it offers visitors the possibility to win big at slots or Blackjack, stay in high quality presidential-style suites, and rub elbows with the rich and famous.

But Las Vegas it is not. Atlantic City hit a huge bump in its road to success. Before gambling was legalized there in 1976, Atlantic City had become a disheveled former resort town where success echoed only in its past. Tourists were sparse, and cash flow was even sparser.

Atlantic City has been a major vacation destination since the late 1800s, with packed trains constantly heading in and out of the city. But starting in the 1940s, tourism began a steady decline, and, following suit, so did the employment rate and population. Something needed to be done. Eventually, legal gambling seemed to be the answer.

But the gambling laws were strict. Among other regulations, gambling was only allowed in hotels with more than 500 rooms. So who stood to benefit from this new onslaught of gambling tourism? Not the local townspeople, and certainly not the local businesses – only large companies with enough corporate assets to afford the massive gambling license requirements and the means to build a hotel of this size. These companies moved to town and reaped all the benefits of the new laws, leaving the locals right where they started.

This resulted in a huge division of the town that is immediately visible to anybody touring the area. On one block is a huge multimillion-dollar resort complex that clearly has lots of money pouring into it. *Directly on the other side of the street* (not a mile down or three blocks away) is a tiny single-family house in dire need of a new paint job. How can this be?

THE CURRENT DESIGN OF ATLANTIC CITY

Atlantic City is two worlds; the resort world and the surrounding community. These two worlds are so vastly different both in design and financial situation that it cannot possibly be a mistake. I speculate: at some point during the re-design, the city's bigwigs probably got together and tried to come up with a way to keep those people visiting to gamble and enjoy the resort totally and completely separate from the rest of the city. From the moment visitors enter the city to the moment they leave, how can they be kept in the casinos and on the boardwalk without straying anywhere else?

The result of this "discussion" is a simple yet brilliant collection of walkway connectors; self-contained parking garages and resort casinos that do a fantastic job of keeping the vacationers within the resorts and out of the rest of the city. If a curious vacationer wished to explore the rest of the city, he or she would first have to navigate unattractive parking lots, trash collection centers and other ugly, perhaps unsafe environments. Each and every resort on the boardwalk adheres to this philosophy: have an easy and comfortable time exploring our resort and the boardwalk, but do not leave. This architectural design and business practice is a marvel of ingenuity, arguably unsurpassable in terms of simplicity and thoughtfulness.

Today's visitors to Atlantic City are well aware of this division, even if not on a conscious level. Many of them come only to gamble, and oftentimes leave without even spending the night. Many come in on buses which drop them off right in front of a casino – they never have to set foot off the resort property. So no tourist money gets placed back into the economy. These people come for the day and many times never even walk out onto the boardwalk. They are dumped into the casino and only leave when they are broke from too much gambling. Not even nearby local businesses get any financial runoff. The only non-casino companies that benefit from any tourism are those with locations directly on the boardwalk, in between casinos – and even those spots are pricey to maintain.

In more recent days, however, private investors have realized that there is money to be made in Atlantic City that does not revolve around gambling. The mechanisms are there to attract tourists; all the city needs is additional off-casino-property activities. Recent additions include an outlet mall, a wax museum, and several famous themed restaurants (all discussed later in this book). In addition, the New Jersey Casino Reinvestment Development Authority (CRDA) has been charged with using funds acquired by gambling to improve the greater Atlantic City and New Jersey areas.

As a resort town, Atlantic City is beautiful. It is an ideal location right on ocean, with many miles of beaches and many days of ideal vacation climate during the hot summertime. Hopefully, this book will help you take advantage of all that Atlantic City has to offer. If you want, you can even gamble a little – but not too much, save some time and money for the real attractions!

CASINO RESORTS

Casino floors are all the same, no matter what hotel they are located in. So, to differentiate one hotel from the next, casinos seem to be using "themes" for their casinos and hotels. This is most apparent in Las Vegas, for example, with one hotel having an Italian theme, another having a circus theme, and another trying for ancient Rome. Atlantic City operates on similar criteria (since many hotel operators in Atlantic City also operate hotels in Las Vegas).

These are themes. They are tacky. They are not real. Many of the decorations are too obviously made of plastic. The huge statue of Augustus Caesar seen in the lobby of Caesars Atlantic City is not real. You know it. I know it. Once somebody gets over the fact that they are not actually in ancient Rome and once somebody stops being angry that a major corporation is pulling a fast one on them by making a fake whatever, that somebody can start enjoying the artistry and the design and the perfection of the tack.

Calling something "tacky" can be a compliment – but it doesn't have to be. Quality tack must maintain a professional look. It must be regularly cleaned and sharp and the lighting scheme must match the drapes. Disney theme parks and hotels are examples of quality tack. *Ripley's Believe it or Not!* Museums, *Pirates Cove Adventure Golf* mini-golf courses, *Planet Hollywood* and *Hard Rock Café* are all examples of quality tack.

At the risk of offending those who attempt quality tack but fail, I won't mention any specifics; but tack that does not meet my standards involves lighting not up to par (lighting schemes are a important when determining the quality of tack), or themes that are not consistent. If colors don't match or the scheme of the environment isn't pleasing, the tack doesn't work.

An unusual example of quality tack: Times Square in New York City. Although all the lights and the signs are so large and gaudy, each sign if hung alone might be construed as bad tack – there is no theme, no consistency; these billboards would be out of place almost anywhere else. However, because there are so many of them in one tiny location, they all overlap each other and crowd the sky so much and with such oppression that suddenly bad tack becomes one of the best, most eclectic examples of quality tack there is.

Quality tack, in many ways, is much like a movie set – everything is designed to create a certain illusion — the lights and the props, the large water fountains in the entry way. Everything works in synergy to create an artificial environment that is perhaps too bright for real life, but just perfect for your vacation.

Atlantic City is all about tack. Gambling – the core of its new beginning – focuses all non-gambling assets on tack. So it is important to realize, when you read the information in this book, that I actually *like* this kind of thing.

My Take on Gambling

I am not a rich man; I cannot afford to invest hundreds of dollars into a slot machine or on a blackjack table with the slim hope that I will hit the jackpot. However, I do enjoy the casino environment. On one of many recent trips to Atlantic City (researching this book), I spent the evening glued to one particular slot machine and perhaps spent about $75 over the course of a few hours. I did not expect to win any jackpot. I had a few complimentary drinks, listened to a band play some of my favorite Meat Loaf hits from the 1970s, and really enjoyed the ambience. Drinking and casinos are a perfect mix; a bit of alcohol really lets you enjoy the repetitive nature of gambling, especially the mindless slots.

But I easily get bored. I can spend several hours with drinks and slots and be perfectly content, but that is $75 down the drain and I will have nothing but a few comp dollars and a slight hangover to show for it. I enjoyed myself, but I wanted more.

This is my feeling towards Atlantic City. I really love the resort environment and the inherent tackiness of casino resort-hotels (as the previous section describes). But I cannot enjoy such a place for long, when the sole purpose is to gamble. I want to enjoy the boardwalk. I want to have a nice buffet lunch and go shopping. I want more than a casino.

That is exactly why I wrote this book. I am not against gambling; in fact I really enjoy it if the situation is right. Atlantic City has the capability to make an entire vacation experience without just slots and table games. Until now, books simply do not exist that describe things in Atlantic City other than the casino environment. My goal is to change that. While Atlantic City doesn't itself have a bad reputation, its name carries with it a connotation that only rich gamblers and desperate paycheck-to-paycheck workers can enjoy the scene. I strongly disagree.

HOW THIS BOOK IS ORGANIZED

This book is divided into two parts: resort attractions and non-resort attractions. While the major draw to the resorts is gambling, there are other things to do in the resorts, such as eating, shopping, catching some live entertainment, dancing all night, and more. The first section will discuss each of Atlantic City's thirteen resorts; what to see, what to do, and where to eat.

The second section covers the rest of Atlantic City. Non-resort activities and attractions are listed by section, based on the type of attraction: amusement centers, entertainment and sports, museums and culture, parks and recreation, shopping, and nightlife. These attractions are listed by name in the table of contents for easy reference.

Finally, there is a listing of select area hotels and restaurants, as well as other useful information for planning your next trip to Atlantic City. Included here are web site addresses, information on family-friendly attractions, area golf courses, and other at-a-glance items.

THE CRAMMER CONCLUSION - THIS BOOK IS PERSONAL

As you may have guessed, this book is much different than other travel guides you may have read. It is an extremely biased look at a resort community that has the potential to be one of the best in the country. I get frustrated because of the publicity and word of mouth that Atlantic City receives. I tell friends that I'm going there for vacation, and they immediately assume I'm a gambler. No. I enjoy the tacky hotels, I enjoy the ocean, I enjoy the amusement parks and the boardwalk and the bars and restaurants and the many other things that make up this wonderful place. Las Vegas it is not, but it damn well could be.

WHY VISIT ATLANTIC CITY?

In the Northeast, there are many popular local vacation destinations. Many New Yorkers may visit The Hamptons near the tip of Long Island. Bostonians may head to Cape Cod, Martha's Vineyard, or Nantucket. Thrill-seekers find their way to one of the Six Flags theme parks in the Northeast, and those looking for a good drive or hike visit the Adirondacks, the Catskills, or the Poconos. But for many in the Mid-Atlantic region, summer is synonymous with the Jersey Shore.

From Sandy Hook to Cape May, New Jersey has turned its Atlantic shoreline into an almost nonstop cavalcade of vacation destinations. From the quaint southern tip of Cape May to amusement-park-crammed Wildwood to the gambling hotspot of Atlantic City, the Jersey Shore is visited by millions of vacationers every year. The variety of activities is endless, with something for just about everyone.

Geographically, the Jersey Shore is actually a series of long, thin islands that run down the eastern coast of the state. Much of these islands are marshland, but the section about a half-mile from the coast is packed with motels, private homes, and various beach and amusement attractions. Many of these towns have their own unique boardwalk that separates the beach from the rest of the city. These boardwalks may be lined with shops, arcades, amusement piers, casinos, or private residences.

For practical purposes, the Jersey Shore is split into two sections – south shore and north shore – by Atlantic City. If one were so inclined, one could actually "island hop" much of the way down the shore by staying off the mainland and using Ocean Drive to drive from island to island. This gives a great overview of what the Jersey Shore has to offer, especially if you plan on vacationing there sometime in the future. Because the Shore is largely the same throughout the 127-mile stretch, most people do not visit the entire length of the Shore; they usually have one specific favorite location they visit year after year.

In general, the Jersey Shore is densely crowded with "bennies" – (shore slang for summertime vacationers) during the summer and becomes almost a series of ghost towns in the winter. The exception to this, of course, is Atlantic City, where much of the attraction is indoors, and tourists visit year-round. If you plan on enjoying the beach, expect to spend some money and compete with thousands of local visitors. A trip in the winter, however, can be a totally different and unique experience.

ATLANTIC CITY HISTORY

If Philadelphia is independence and New York is commerce, Atlantic City is vacation! Located on Absecon Island, a thin stretch of land on the Atlantic Ocean about 10 miles long and separated from the mainland by 6 miles of uninhabitable swamp, Atlantic City has been a favorite summertime destination for centuries. Long before European settlers claimed the land, it was a heavily forested area which served as home for the Lenni-Lenape Native Americans. Their name for the island, Absegami, means "little water," indicating the thin expanse of water separating it from the mainland. The island was largely ignored, even after New Jersey had attained statehood in 1787, because it was inaccessible from the mainland except by boat.

By 1800, Jonathon Leeds became the first permanent resident of the island. Fifty years later, only a few others had joined his descendants as residents (Leeds himself had died in the 1830s), and the community grew slowly. As these first years progressed, the name of the island was changed to Absecum, then later to Absecon.

It was Dr. Jonathon Pitney, a recent graduate of a prestigious New York college, who saw the future of Absecon Island as a major tourist destination. By 1852, he and a group of businessmen had secured the rights to build the Camden-Atlantic railroad, which would stretch from Camden, a city near Philadelphia, to Absecon Island. In a mood of corporate loyalty, Richard Osbourne, a railway engineer who helped design the basic layout, christened the railroad's destination "Atlantic City". Osbourne and Pitney together also designed the new city's streets; roads heading north-south would be named after bodies of water (Pacific, Baltic, Mediterranean, etc), and roads heading east-west would be named after states (Tennessee, South Carolina, Pennsylvania, etc).

Atlantic City was incorporated in March of 1854, and that same year the first train made its way down the new line. The total trip of about 60 miles took 2.5 hours, but by the trip's end, as the first vacationers stepped off the train and onto the beach, the era of Atlantic City tourism had begun.

After 1860, Atlantic City became one of the hottest vacation destinations in America. Its primary draw – location – made it accessible from several major urban areas, particularly Philadelphia. People from all over would flock to the city's beaches to enjoy summer activities. At the time, Atlantic City focused its energies on being a health resort. Doctors would even prescribe the city's "sea air" as a remedy for stress, pain, and even insanity. As the population and tourism grew, the businesses began to expand and move closer to the beach.

There was only one problem with the close proximity to the beach – the beach itself. Merchants were inundated with sand dragged, dropped and otherwise deposited in their establishments. In the late 1860s, railroad constructor Andrew Boardman proposed a solution. Along with others, he suggested a walkway that would rise above the sand and allow beachgoers to clean their feet before leaving the beach. On June 26, 1870, the plan was realized – a wooden walkway was completed that separated the beach from the rest of the city. Boardman's Walk – as it was called – was the world's first. The name was eventually shortened to "boardwalk". As demand for additional beachfront space rose, the boardwalk grew. This expansion led to the invention in 1884 of another Atlantic City staple, the rolling chair. A canopied chair designed to be pushed from behind, it made traveling the length of the ever-expanding boardwalk easier for wealthy vacationers.

Boardwalk real estate became a prime location. All sorts of beachside attractions sprang up, from amusement piers to sideshows to performance theaters to small vendors selling Salt Water Taffy (another Atlantic City first) and more. Steeplechase Pier, Steel Pier, Heinz Pier, the Million Dollar Pier, and others made their glorious debuts in those first few decades of rapid development.

Between 1890 and 1940, Atlantic City's history becomes less a single chain of events, but rather a series of "oddities" and "firsts." So much happened in Atlantic City during its heyday: presidents came to speak, magicians dazzled audiences, amusement piers came and went and came again, and countless other bits and pieces of history were made. Atlantic City had razzle-dazzle, craziness, in-your-face showiness, corporate enterprising, and everything in between.

The first picture postcards in the U.S. were views of Atlantic City in 1872. Salt Water Taffy was invented and named there around 1880. The first air-conditioned theater opened in the summer of 1896. Although Chicago holds fame for the first "Ferris Wheel," it was in 1891 that Williams Somers built an "observational roundabout" on the boardwalk. It was this wheel ride that was observed and improved upon by George Washington Gale Ferris for the 1893 Chicago World's Fair, and it is his name, not Somers', that is today attached to the ride.

The string of "firsts" continued into the 20th century. In 1915, the first non-subsidized public transportation system, The Atlantic City Jitney, was established. The first passenger airline service made its way through Atlantic City in 1919, the same year that the term "airport" was coined. Of course, the Miss America pageant started here in 1921, and continues to this day. The first official convention hall opened its doors in Atlantic City in 1929. For golfers, the slang terms "Eagle" and "Birdie" were first used here.

By 1944, the Atlantic City Boardwalk stretched a staggering seven miles down the coast of Absecon Island – ending in Longport, three cities south. However, in the fall of that year, a massive east coast hurricane destroyed most of the boardwalk, many attractions and several amusement piers. The Boardwalk would eventually be rebuilt to a shorter distance of about 5.75 miles (including the Ventnor section).

The hurricane of 1944 may have been the straw that broke the proverbial camel's back for Atlantic City tourism. Commercial airline travel, popularized in the 1930s and 1940s, was making exotic destinations (such as Florida and the Bahamas) more accessible. There was less need for a local vacation destination, and Atlantic City tourism began its

Atlantic City: Beyond Gambling 25

steady decline. By the 1960s, Atlantic City was dead. With almost no tourist income, high unemployment, and low population, something needed to be done.

-The New Face of Atlantic City -

In 1970, a bill was introduced to the New Jersey Assembly suggesting the legalization of gambling statewide as a way to boost Atlantic City's economy. The bill was rejected and the idea dropped, partly due to pressure from protest groups against the idea of legalized gambling in New Jersey. At that point, the only state in the U.S. with legalized gambling was Nevada (established in the 1930s). Three similar gambling bills were brought to the assembly before it was finally approved in 1976, and only after the bill was modified to allow for gambling exclusively in Atlantic City, and not statewide as the previous proposals has suggested. A mere 18 months later, in May 1978, the first casino in Atlantic City – Resorts International – opened its doors. In the ensuing years, other casinos quickly followed suit, and a new wave of tourism began.

Legalizing gambling in Atlantic City was meant to revitalize an economically and socially stagnant area. Since 1976, revenues and tourism have skyrocketed, from virtually no tourism to well over 30 million visitors each year. The money generated from gambling was intended, in part, to be invested into the community as dictated in the Casino Control Act of 1977. For years, however, little progress was made in the way of the city's revitalization. Until recently, it appeared that casino revenue went right back into the resort.

The Casino Control Act is largely responsible for the way Atlantic City operates today. Many of the activities and cultural attractions available to visitors exist almost exclusively because of this addendum to the New Jersey state law. The Act dictates how gambling funds are distributed and how casinos should operate. Those who enjoy Atlantic City's diverse cultural activities, entertainment, and historical monuments should be aware that gambling revenues largely influence their preservation and development. The Casino Control Act functions as follows:

The New Jersey Constitution expressly says that the state is in charge of the gambling in Atlantic City. To that effect, the Casino Control Act created the **New Jersey Casino Control Commission** (Tennessee Avenue & Boardwalk, Atlantic City, NJ, information: 609-441-3799, http://www.state.nj.us/casinos/). The commission has been charged with the regulation of gambling within New Jersey, and specifically Atlantic City. The office is in charge of licenses, employment, permits, and other issues pertaining to casino gambling. Casino Control Commission offices are located in each of the casino resorts in Atlantic City on the casino floor, and readily accessible for walk-in information or complaints. The **New Jersey Department of Gaming Enforcement** (P.O. Box 047, Trenton, NJ, http://www.njdge.org), a division of the Office of Law & Public Safety, ensures that the laws and regulations set forth by the state and commission are met.

According to the Casino Control Act, in order to operate a casino within Atlantic City, the following conditions apply: (1) the casino must operate in a hotel with at least 500 rooms of 325 square feet per room or more, (2) the casino floor must be no more than 60,000 square feet. (3) For each additional 100 rooms, the casino floor may expand 10,000 square feet, up to a total of 200,000 square feet. (4) The hotel must be, in the words of the Casino Control Act, a "superior, first-class facility of exceptional quality which will help restore Atlantic City as a resort, tourist and convention destination." In addition, the commission has the authority to alter the rules of any casino game, including dictate odds, set bet sizes or change payout structure.

Atlantic City's casinos gross around forty million dollars each and every month. Much of this money goes back into the maintenance of the resorts, but a portion must be invested in the economy of New Jersey. This is the job of the **Casino Reinvestment Development Authority** (1014 Atlantic Avenue, Atlantic City, NJ, 609-347-0500). Created in 1984, the Authority is designed to utilize casino revenue to "give back" to the community by initiating various projects and to create public confidence in the value of casino gambling.

Such projects of the CRDA include partnerships with the Ocean Life Center, the Absecon Lighthouse, Sandcastle Stadium, and the Korean War Memorial. Various neighborhoods in Atlantic City and the rest of New Jersey have received help from the CRDA. It is through many of these projects and partnerships that Atlantic City has made a major comeback in recent years, in terms of both the local community and the tourism business.

The Casino Control Act also provides compulsive gamblers or

Atlantic City: Beyond Gambling

any who feel they have a gambling problem the opportunity to be voluntarily placed on an exclusion list. Called the **Self-Exclusion Program**, participants may elect to place themselves on a list distributed to the casinos, which would prevent them from gambling for a specified period of time. Those on the list cannot collect winnings, receive complimentary items from casinos, or apply for casino credit.

To the credit of the Casino Control Act and its creators, Atlantic City has seen a sudden boom in commerce and a second life. The progress has been slow but steady, and each year sees an increase in tourism and activities. One day Atlantic City may be known not just for tourism and gambling, but for the local community as well. Today, the 10-mile stretch of Absecon Island is home to several communities. In addition to Atlantic City, the island also supports the communities Margate, Ventnor, and Longport. Though these communities do not have the historical importance or commercial draw of Atlantic City, they have all at some point contributed to – or benefited from - Atlantic City's astonishing success. The main hub of commerce on the island is still the boardwalk; over 31 million visitors make their way there every year.

Today, according to the 2000 census, there are 40,517 people residing on the 11.4 square miles of land in Atlantic City. Of these, the majority of the racial make-up consists of Black or African American (44.16%) and White or Caucasian (26.68%). More than a quarter (25.7%) of the population is under the age of 18, and 14.2% are over 65. The household income is $26,969, with 23.6% living below the poverty line. On the other hand, tourist makeup is a different story. Visitors will notice a high population of senior citizens in the resorts and casinos, and very few children. Most of the younger set – in the summertime, anyway - find their way to other places on the Jersey Shore. But Atlantic City is making a huge comeback; with much more for families and resort enthusiasts than just a few years ago.

The days of classic Atlantic City are long gone, replaced with a different kind of modern glitz. But gone is not forgotten. To experience turn-of-the-century Atlantic City, as it was in its heyday, consider making a visit to the **Walt Disney World** resort in Florida (407-W-DISNEY, http://www.disneyworld.com). In one resort, Disney has re-created the ambience of the original Atlantic City. Disney's BoardWalk, a AAA Four-Star Diamond resort, features much of what Atlantic City used to be. In addition to a nice boardwalk stroll, guests can bike, play midway games, eat, drink, dance, and be merry until the wee hours of the morning (Of course, pay no attention to Epcot's Spaceship Earth, which peaks over the horizon).

THINGS TO SEE AND DO

Atlantic City is the only area on the Jersey Shore that sees tourists consistently year-round. The casinos – the main draw – are entirely indoors. But many of the non-casino-based activities are open year-round, so a trip to Atlantic City can be fun whenever you plan on visiting.

- The Beach and Boardwalk -

The beach, of course, is the largest attraction – it's what Atlantic City was named for, and the reason it exists at all! Access to the beach is very generous; you can walk right up to the ocean from one of many access points on the boardwalk. You can sunbathe or swim, but keep in mind that this portion of the Jersey Shore is largely lifeguard-free, so you may be on your own. The beach is regularly cleaned and maintained, and although it's not the Bahamas, it is well-kept and there are miles and miles of it. And the best part is, unlike other parts of the Jersey Shore, access to Atlantic City's beach is always free!

The Atlantic City Boardwalk lines about 5.75 miles of beach. Most resorts populate only a 2-3 mile stretch of this famous walk. In between them are countless small souvenir shops, video arcades, and various food and gift stands. Many hotels also have outdoor bars that are open during nicer weather. As is to be expected, a vast majority of the attractions in Atlantic City are located on the boardwalk, but that doesn't mean you shouldn't go exploring!

- Resort Hotels -

Atlantic City is home to thirteen massive resort hotels, each with its own unique flair. They all have multiple dining facilities, entertainment and shopping opportunities, and most have some kind of performance or convention hall. Ten of the resorts are located on the boardwalk and the remaining three are in the nearby Marina District. And of course, they all have large casinos.

From Atlantic City to Las Vegas to cruise ships to Native American reservations, casinos all have a similar appearance. They are basically huge rooms filled with slots, table games, bars, and special parlors for high-limit gamblers. Craps, blackjack, roulette, baccarat, and poker are staples of table games, and slot machines offer every imaginable way of spinning wheels to match symbols.

But Atlantic City is unique in a way that separates it from most other gambling destinations – it is not founded on gambling. People flocked to the seaside resort long, *long* before gambling was a gleam even in the eyes of Las Vegas; a city not yet founded (Las Vegas was incorporated in 1911, gambling was legalized there in 1931). They would come from miles around to stroll along the boardwalk, lie on the beach, and enjoy summer life. So Atlantic City is not historically a gambling town; gambling is a very recent occurrence.

- Amusement Centers -

Like California, the Jersey Shore is famous for its amusement piers - attractions stretching out onto the beach and sometimes even over the ocean. The Shore has many such piers; some large and well known, others smaller and more intimate. But they all offer much the same experience – a stroll down the boardwalk with cotton candy and stomach-churning, thrill-inducing midway rides.

In Atlantic City today, there are a total of four "official" amusement piers at fairly evenly spaced intervals on the resort section of the boardwalk. Historically, however, there have been many more piers that have come and gone in the early decades of the 1900s. Heinz Pier and Steeplechase Pier have gone the way of the winds, but The Million Dollar Pier (today Ocean Pier, or "The Pier at Caesars"), Central Pier (on the spot of the nation's first amusement pier), and Steel Pier have stood the test of time, albeit undergoing repairs and major restorations over the years.

- Entertainment and Sports -

Baseball, football, hockey. Miss America and Boardwalk Hall. Miniature Golf and outdoor festivities. All of these are right within your grasp in

Atlantic City. Freeskate in a year-round, indoor ice skating facility. Check out a minor league Atlantic City Surf baseball game. Enjoy summertime jazz concerts or play mini-golf directly on the boardwalk. Check out the annual Miss America pageant and finals at the historic Boardwalk Convention Hall. Prefer "real" golf? The Atlantic City area has many golf courses, both public and private, both for daily use and for members only.

- Parks and Recreation -

In addition to the beach and the ocean, there are other places to relax — and get back to nature — in Atlantic City. The New Jersey Pine Barrens are just around the corner, and the Wharton State Forest is New Jersey's largest. Just a few miles inland, you can enjoy a hike, canoe ride, camping trip, bike ride, picnic — just about anything you can imagine doing in the Great Outdoors.

For coastal bird watching and habitat exploration, the Edwin B. Forsythe National Wildlife Refuge is the perfect place to visit. And it's also only a short drive up the coast from Atlantic City. If you're more into water exploration, Gardner's Basin is a departure point for several area day-cruises, which include fishing or sight-seeing expeditions. Lakes Bay — part of the marshy expanse that separates Absecon Island from the mainland — is a windsurfer's paradise.

- Shopping and Nightlife -

The Atlantic City area is jam-packed with shopping possibilities, both within the major resorts or outside. From retail department stores to small gift shops to outlet malls and everything in between, chances are you'll find what you're looking for in one of the area's many shopping centers. Some resorts offer plentiful shopping, some even house entire retail malls. But there is much to buy beyond the boardwalk, with establishments ranging from quaint shopping villages to massive indoor multi-level suburban malls.

After hours, prepare for your night-owl nature to take over. All casinos are open 24 hours a day, and several of the resorts host fine dance clubs and 24-hour restaurants. Atlantic City's nightlife is both famous and infamous, so venture off the boardwalk to find some key

Jersey Shore hotspots and clubs where the party lasts all night.

GETTING TO ATLANTIC CITY

Atlantic City's close proximity to several large population centers has been a major factor in its development as a vacation destination. Washington, D.C. is about 180 miles away. New York City is 128 miles away. Philadelphia is a mere 60 miles away. If you don't plan on driving, the Atlantic City International Airport, with services from several major airline carriers, is less than 10 miles away. Atlantic City is very friendly towards private bus charters (most resorts have a bus terminal on-property) so taking a bus is a great and inexpensive alternative to driving.

- From Points North -

Atlantic City is best accessed via the Garden State Parkway in New Jersey. The Parkway is easily reached from various southbound routes, particularly I-95 if your starting point is either New York City or north. In any case, connect to the Parkway heading southbound as soon as it becomes available. This major highway winds down the east coast of the state and is the main thoroughfare for accessing all points along the Jersey Shore. Frequent travelers of the Parkway either love it or hate it. It requires several toll stops, and sometimes it can be extremely crowded (especially during the summer months when the Jersey Shore is bustling with activity), but it is a well-maintained and attractive stretch that has a very forested look (especially to anyone leaving the congested Jersey Turnpike/I-95 area around New York City). The mile markers on the Parkway count down to 0 (ending at Cape May, the southern tip of the state), and the Atlantic City Expressway is at exit/mile 38.

From New York City via the Garden State Parkway—assuming minimal traffic—the trip will take about 2.5 hours. However, for a much slower route (yet with more scenic beauty) US Route 9 parallels the Parkway almost all the way (and continues down the coast beyond New Jersey). It is a two-lane local road that takes you through many small New Jersey towns and gives a nice perspective of the north-Jersey Shore area, but the drive can be in excess of four to five hours from New York City. Finally, if you want to delay your trip even more, but want the best possible view of the Jersey Shore, take Ocean Drive – a series of roads that allows you to drive along the center of the many islands that make up the Shore. Ocean Drive is not a direct route, however, and it will make frequent stops and sometimes lead you back to the mainland and out to the Shore again.

From whatever route you decide traveling south, you will eventually have to turn east for the final leg of the trip. Direct access to Atlantic City is on the Atlantic City Expressway, exit 38, which will take you past the Atlantic City Welcome Center and directly to the midtown boardwalk resort area. However, if you are not staying in a boardwalk resort or hotel, you may want to consider taking exits 40 or 37. Exit 40 takes you to the Marina District via US Route 30 / White Horse Pike / Absecon Boulevard, which is home to many hotels and offers a stunning view of the Atlantic City Skyline across the vast marshy coastal wetlands separating Absecon Island from the mainland. Exit 37 takes you to US Route 40 / Black Horse Pike, which is another major hotel section that eventually takes you next to Lakes Bay (the *Accommodations* section has more information on hotels in these areas).

- From Points East and South –

Traveling from Philadelphia is simply a matter of negotiating your way onto the Atlantic City Expressway and then holding tight for about 60 miles until you reach the boardwalk. This expressway is along the original route that the first railroad heading to Atlantic City was located. Atlantic City is the closest shore point to Philadelphia, which is the primary reason Atlantic City exists today. As a result, most traffic comes in and out of the city via this expressway. For Philadelphians, however, speed to the shore is traded for the more scenic route that upstate vacationers have. The tolled Atlantic City Expressway is simply a matter of getting to the shore, with little diversion along the way.

Cape May on the southern tip of New Jersey is a dead end. Without taking a seventy-plus-minute ferry or driving the long way around the Delaware Bay, you cannot access the Garden State Parkway or Atlantic City. So the best option is to find your way to the Atlantic City Expressway. This is easiest to access via I-95, which runs all the way up and down the east coast of the country (from Maine to Miami). After connecting to the Atlantic City Expressway from I-95, the drive is an additional 50 miles east to the boardwalk.

- Taking the Bus -

If you live in a major urban area, such as New York City or Philadelphia, you may have the option of using one of several bus lines' casino junkets, such as those offered by **Greyhound** (1-800-229-9424, http://www.greyhound.com). Private bus companies offer greatly reduced fares on a round-trip casino bus ticket, and even a casino bonus (generally equitable to cash) upon arrival. Though these casino bus routes are geared towards gamblers, you do not actually have to gamble. Plus, because of the city's layout, much is accessible by walking directly from the boardwalk resorts, so you may not even need a car! Of course, a car is a necessity if you wish to explore the surrounding area (and many of the attractions in this book), or don't want to spend a good portion of your day walking up and down the two-plus mile boardwalk resort area.

Bus service to Atlantic City casinos varies depending on departure city. There may be 5 buses a day or one every fifteen minutes. In New York City (from Port Authority Bus Terminal), there can be as many as 30-40 buses a day, so you can go to Atlantic City almost whenever you want. If you live in a major urban area (particularly New York City, but also Philadelphia, Washington D.C., or Baltimore, Maryland), check with your local bus service to see what kind of casino packages they offer. With the proper research and combination of low fares and casino bonuses, people can get round-trip tickets to Atlantic City for a little as $8-$10.

- By Air -

A mere 10 miles from the boardwalk via the Atlantic City Expressway is The **Atlantic City International Airport** (Egg Harbor Township, 609-645-7895, http://www.acairport.com, airport code: ACY). The airport services several popular commercial airlines, as well as charters, and even a heliport. Taxi and shuttle services may be available to bring you to the resort area. In addition, there are rental car agencies located within the airport, including Hertz, Avis, and Budget.

- By Train -

Philadelphians have lucked out — they can use the Atlantic City Line of the **New Jersey Transit** (http://www.njtransit.com) to quickly reach the shore with minimal hassle. The Atlantic City train station is within walking distance to the boardwalk and the midtown resort area (but there are frequent resort shuttles available if one so chooses). The station is attached to the new Atlantic City Convention Center and right across the street from the **Sheraton Hotel** (2 Miss America Way, Atlantic City, NJ, 609-344-3535) - the largest non-casino hotel in Atlantic City, which caters to conventioneers.

Though access to Atlantic City via train from New York City is possible, travelers would be forced to transfer trains at least twice (unless they use **Amtrak** (1-800-USA-RAIL, http://www.amtrak.com), at more than triple the price — and they would still have to transfer in Philadelphia). Plus, the trip could take in excess of five hours. In this case, a train may be fun, but its expensive and time-consuming.

GETTING AROUND ATLANTIC CITY

A majority of the resorts are located on a two-mile stretch of boardwalk, directly on the beach of the Atlantic Ocean. So walking between these resorts is a definite and common possibility. But if a long beachfront walk is not your thing, or if you want to explore beyond the boardwalk resorts, you're going to need to secure some kind of transportation alternative to your walking shoes. If you have a car, all resorts have extensive indoor parking garages (many charge a daily use parking fee from between $2 and $4, and sometimes you can even use several resorts' garages for one daily fee).

Driving between boardwalk resorts is accomplished via either Atlantic Avenue or Pacific Avenue, which parallels the beach. Traffic on these roads can be heavy especially during peak travel times, but since the distances between resorts are not very far, it's generally easy to reach your destination. For resorts in the Marina District, the Atlantic City Connector, accessible right off the Atlantic City Expressway is the easiest way to go back and forth between resort areas. If you are exploring non-resort areas, much of the city is on a grid. However, in the northernmost section of the City, near Gardner's Basin, some streets run diagonal, so a navigational map might be necessary.

- Traveling by Jitney -

The **Atlantic City Jitney Association** (201 Pacific Avenue, 609-344-8642, http://www.acjitney.com) was established in 1915, and today is the longest running mass transportation company that is not government-subsidized in the United States. The company operates small, 13-passenger motor coaches that make regular stops at the city's more popular tourist destinations, including all the resorts, the Absecon Lighthouse, the Railroad Station, Gardner's Basin, City Hall, the library, as well as the hospital and police station. The Jitney is very popular and stops very frequently 24 hours a day, seven days a week.

Jitney routes are color-coded and all routes intersect Pacific Avenue, so you should have little trouble finding the right route along this well-beaten path. Your hotel or resort host will have information about where to access the Jitney, and about routes and destinations. The Jitney fare is $1.50 per single ride (payable in cash only upon boarding), but you can purchase bulk frequent rider tickets and save a few cents.

- Traveling by Taxi -

Atlantic City public taxis are abundant, particularly at the major resorts and attractions. Taxi fares are expensive, but if you travel within the city limits the fare caps at $8 (plus tip), so you will not have to spend more than that (most taxi fares around town will wind up being about $8). Taxis can also be taken from the Atlantic City Airport, but the fare is significantly higher than trips around town.

- Traveling By Rolling Chair -

Almost as old as the boardwalk itself, the rolling chairs in Atlantic City are as much a staple of the city's history as they are a fun and convenient way to get around the boardwalk. For a per-minute fee, up to three guests at a time can literally be pushed around on small, enclosed chairs as they are calmly brought to their boardwalk destination. Though not much faster than walking (the chairs are, after all, pushed) they allow you to sit and enjoy the sites. The rolling chairs also operate year-round, with small plastic screens shielding the riders from the winter winds. As recently as April of 2002, **Royal Rolling Chairs** (114 S. New York Ave, Atlantic City, NJ, 609-347-7500, http://www.rollingchairs.com) was established.

Spending the Night in Atlantic City

When deciding to spend the night in Atlantic City, there is one critical question you must ask yourself: *will you be staying on-resort or off-resort?* There are two worlds to Atlantic City commerce – on one side there are huge resort-hotels, and on the other side there is the rest of the city. There are clear disadvantages and advantages to each class of accommodation, so make sure you know what you are getting into before booking that room.

If you are staying on-resort, chances are you'll be paying top-dollar for your room, which may cost upwards of $400 on a busy summer weekend (but can cost as low as $50 if you shop around). You'll be in a high quality resort, large and clean, with many on-site restaurants and shops. You'll probably be in a prime location, most likely on the boardwalk. Of course, directly within your hotel will be a large, clean, and always bustling casino. You may not need a car to get around or enjoy your vacation, since there will be much to do well within walking distance. Additionally, resort hotels offer many levels of suites. Some have fitness centers, a pool, spa, or health facility. However, these facilities may have additional cost.

If you are staying off-resort, the quality, price, and location of your hotel or motel will vary significantly. You will probably not be on the boardwalk, and you may not even be near the boardwalk. However, your hotel/motel may offer limited shuttle service to the closest resort. You will be paying less for your room, and may have easier access to the off-boardwalk attractions. The hotel may have a restaurant, pool, health spa, or other amenities on-site, but most do not. Also, rooms off-site do not fill up as quickly, so they may be a better option for last-minute vacations.

Since Atlantic City's busiest season is the summer, you can save a lot of money by visiting in the wintertime. You won't be able to enjoy some attractions, such as Steel Pier (Atlantic City's amusement park), but many other local attractions will be available for your entertainment. Additionally, on weekends room prices soar to about three to four times the weekday rate, and sometimes rooms are unavailable in general. During the busiest times (especially summer holidays), even the most aesthetically questionable of motels may be sold out.

There are several ways to book your hotel room. Most chain hotels (including the resorts) have their own website, and mostly you can book online from there. These sites may have special deals or packages not available elsewhere. You can also use a travel agent such as **Travelocity** (1-888-709-5983, http://www.travelocity.com) or **hotels.com** (1-800-246-8357, http://www.hotels.com). However, if you need specific accommodations, such as suites, it's recommended you call the resort or hotel directly.

LOCAL PUBLICATIONS - WHERE TO FIND THE LATEST INFO

The best resource for Atlantic City tourism is the **Atlantic City Convention & Visitor's Authority** (2314 Pacific Avenue, Atlantic City, NJ, 1-888-AC-VISIT http://www.atlanticcitynj.com). With one location on the Atlantic City Expressway (mile marker 2.5) and one on the boardwalk directly adjacent to Boardwalk Hall, The Bureau is a veritable potpourri of various pamphlets, entertainment and resort listings, and many attractions. It is a promotional service with funds provided by both the state of New Jersey and by the advertisers that use their services. Similarly, the **Atlantic City Chamber of Commerce** (1125 Atlantic Avenue, Atlantic City, NJ, 609-345-4524, http://www.atlanticcitychamber.com) is closely tied with the Convention & Visitors Authority, with an emphasis on promotion as opposed to tourism.

For current, time-specific information about events, concerts, and advertisements pertinent to Atlantic City and vicinity, there are several local publications available. The largest and oldest free publication in the area is **The Atlantic City Weekly** (8025 Black Horse Pike, Suite 350, West Atlantic City, NJ, 609-646-4848, http://www.acweekly.com), which is available throughout the city at various information kiosks, including most resorts and hotels. While the paper contains some local news and current events, these stories are undermined by the plethora of advertisements pertaining to local attractions, touring shows and show times, restaurants, bars, and classifieds.

For a more traditional print publication, the daily **Press of Atlantic City** (1000 W. Washington Ave, Pleasantville, NJ, 609-272-4000, http://www.pressofatlanticcity.com) features local and national news stories, as well as classifieds, advertisements, and area information. The paper offers a subscription, or can be purchased for 50 cents at a newsstand.

The monthly magazine **Dan Klein's South Jersey Insider** (P.O. Box 829, Ocean City, NJ, 609-398-0624, http://www.shorelinker.com) also contains local entertainment and attraction information, as well as news articles focused on local interests and information. Except for special events, the information in this magazine (available for free at tourist kiosks or by paid subscription) tends to be similar month after month, as the attractions listed don't change monthly. But it is good to keep up to date with prices, operating hours, and such.

There are numerous other publications available for South Jersey and Atlantic City information. Check with your hotel reception desk upon arrival for the latest information.

About 75% of Atlantic City tourists live less than two hundred miles away (namely New York, Philadelphia, and Washington, DC). In recent years, the median age of the tourists dropped from 55 to 52.

Atlantic City in Winter

One of the oddest experiences you can have in Atlantic City is to visit in mid-winter and walk out onto the boardwalk in the middle of the night. It will be completely deserted; you will hear the ocean waves crashing, the lights from the casino will brighten up the boardwalk and the music from the outdoor speakers will be blaring. There is nothing quite like it, anywhere.

Emily Wang, a visitor to Atlantic City, has this to say about her wintertime experience in this predominantly summertime resort area:

"Mention Atlantic City and an image of a deserted boardwalk in the dead of winter comes to my mind. That was how I saw Atlantic City for the first time. The beach dotted with thick patches of icy snow, crisscrossed with the tracks of numerous heavy vehicles. The ocean rougher and wilder than it is in the summer – almost alive in contrast to the still, desolate beach. The air thin and fresh and the wind cruel and biting and heavily spiced with the smell of salt and frost. All up and down the beach and boardwalk nothing but the grey sky and the roaring ocean and the cold, turbulent air. Walking along the boardwalk, steel-gated storefronts and empty restaurants sit dormant and waiting for spring. The casinos and their flashy signs and neon lighting stand dwarfed and mute against the winter, while inside, ringing, clanging and singing machines buzz with activity, oblivious to the season.

"If I let my mind wander through the months, I can see Atlantic City as it is in the summer. The boardwalk is engulfed in a sea of people. The hot, humid air smells of salt and sweat and the smoke off the open air grills of the restaurants lining the beachfront. The carnival atmosphere is noisy, sweltering, and at times, suffocating. Locals out for the day mix with tourists posing for photographs, and the whole jumble of people move en masses towards some unknown destination, up and down the boardwalk, in and out of casinos, restaurants and shops. Vendors hawk everything from popcorn and cotton candy to electronics and CDs. The beach is crawling with bodies. Umbrellas and beach chairs and towels cater to hundreds of tanners, surfers, swimmers, and others that defy categorization. It is a far cry and a distant world from the silent landscape of February.

"I do not go to Atlantic City for the gambling. I like the glitzy fakeness of the casino architecture, and the active hum of the casino floors. I like the opulence and excess of the buffets, lobbies and slot machines. I like the vacation feel of everything. And I like it in winter. I like that you don't have to share the boardwalk and beach with thousands of other people, and I like stepping from the smoky, noisy, chaotic casino into the quiet stillness of the boardwalk. The dichotomy of the two environments is enchanting, and I love that in no other season can you step in from such an open, empty world into one so warm and alive."

ON-RESORT

The Atlantic City Resorts

The main tourist attractions in Atlantic City are located on a two-mile stretch of the world famous **Atlantic City Boardwalk** (the first boardwalk in the country). On the southern end is the Atlantic City Hilton, and on the northern end is Harrah's Showboat. In this section, we will walk up the boardwalk through the entire two-mile stretch and explore the area's chief tourist attractions.

The other major resort section of Atlantic City, called the **Marina District**, is home to three resort-hotels that do not have immediate beach access, and can't be gotten to by walking. Major traffic into the Marina District travels from the boardwalk via the Atlantic City Connector, a short stretch of road, which is partially underground. It allows ultra-fast access and the ability to by-pass the rest of Atlantic City – another way to control tourist access.

All major traffic into Atlantic City comes from the west on the Atlantic City Expressway, which starts in Philadelphia and stretches all the way to the ocean, with major connectors for I-95 and the Garden State Parkway (for points upstate and in New York).

As you arrive on the Atlantic City Expressway, you'll get a great view of the backs of most of the resorts. That's right! Unlike most other types of resorts, those in Atlantic City require that you enter through their back entrance! Why is this? The fronts of the buildings face the ocean. This is true for many buildings located on beachfront property; you will not be able to see the resort for what it is until you walk out onto the boardwalk.

Although most of the hubbub revolves around the resorts themselves, there is much to see in the sections between the hotels (small gift shops and video game arcades and even several amusement piers). These will all be noted as we walk up the boardwalk.

Choosing Your Resort

If you intend to stay in one of these resort hotels, the task of deciding where to book your reservation may seem daunting. Although most resorts are located within a single two-mile line (and you can easily walk between them, sometimes without even stepping outdoors), where you stay is definitely going to be a factor in how much you enjoy yourself.

Before you cram these pages and nervously make that reservation phone call, know this – all of the resorts listed in this section are fine quality, and they all have substantial similarities. You're not going to get treated like a king in one and a pauper in another. Each resort has the following:

1. **Casinos** – Each of these resorts has at least one large casino, filled with all kinds of slot machines and table games. They all have high-limit and regular games. Don't worry; you'll be able to gamble however you want at all of them.
2. **Adequate Parking** – Park yourself or use valet. Parking your car in a resort's self-park lot is the only real value in Atlantic City.
3. **Rooms and Suites** – Each resort has a wide range of accommodations, from standard rooms to the most luxurious of suites. Sometimes these suites are available for booking online, others you will have to call the resort directly.
4. **Restaurants** – No matter where you stay, there will be several on-site restaurants, ranging from 24-hour deli food to fast food to expensive lavish dinner experiences. Of course, they each have that all-important buffet as well.

However, the resorts vary substantially on the following, so it would be best if you planned your trip based on these criteria:

1. **Immediate Beach Access** – Some resorts do NOT have access to the boardwalk and some do not have beach amenities (such as a bar on the beach). Though most resorts do have beach access, you should check, as you'd probably be fairly upset if you packed all your beach toys and found out you had to take a car to get to the beach.
2. **Shopping and Entertainment** – Though all resorts have shopping and entertainment venues, what is offered will vary. Some resorts have popular chain restaurants that you may like, for example.
3. **Proximity to Non-Resort Entertainment** – As this book will discuss, there is an array of things to do in Atlantic City that do not revolve around the resorts. Decide what attractions you are most interested in and stay near them (remember though that everything is generally nearby; so if you aren't right next door there's not much to worry about).
4. **Personal Resort Preference** – Stayed in Caesars Las Vegas? Own stock in the Hilton? Stay in their Atlantic City homes!

The following sections will describe each of the main Atlantic City resort-hotels both on the **Boardwalk** and in the **Marina District**. These are the major draws of Atlantic City. What constitutes a "resort-hotel?" For the purposes of this book, when a hotel contains a casino, it is automatically upgraded to a resort. There are many other hotels in Atlantic City, which are described elsewhere. Atlantic City resort-hotels are home to numerous entertainment and dining options. All restaurants, activities and attractions within a resort are listed here; attractions off resort property (that is, somewhere else in the city) are separated into other sections.

The next chapters are broken down by resort or attraction, starting with those along the boardwalk, and then the other districts of the Atlantic City area. It lists reviews of the hotels, the best way to arrive and experience everything.

Introduction: You will be introduced to the resort, including various facts that first-time travelers should know about the property, the history, and the company behind it.

Arriving at the Hotel: First impressions mean a lot, but as many people going to Atlantic City arrive by bus just to gamble, there are sub-par bus terminals that serve merely to connect the casino to the street. This section will help you avoid these areas and get the right first impression. When of note, this section will also acquaint you with each resort's hotel lobby (a <u>very</u> important factor in quality tackiness).

Accommodations: Although all the resorts listed here (unless otherwise specified) achieve a certain level of quality in their rooms and suites, there are notable differences. This section will discuss the resort's hotel-centered facilities.

Activities: What should one do at any given resort, without gambling? Everything from interesting walks to shopping to non-gaming attractions; this section describes what makes each of the resorts unique. Remember, though, that a vacation destination does not have to require you to do anything – the ambience of a location can play an important factor in your experience. Just sitting and enjoying a situation can be as rewarding as participating.

Entertainment: Looking for some live music or a comedy club? Is there a big event or small intimate entertainment experience? This section explains the resort-hotel's entertainment venue. Any non-activity-based offerings will be described here.

Dining: Each resort has a selection of bars and restaurants on the property. These establishments vary in terms of price, ambience, and more. This section highlights these restaurants – generally from most to least expensive.

THE BOARDWALK RESORTS

America's First Boardwalk. Since the late 1800s, people have been flocking from all over the east coast to this vacation destination to bask in the sun, walk on the beach, shop or play on the boardwalk. It is the centerpiece of Atlantic City, and perhaps of the entire Jersey Shore. It is the jewel around which the rest of Atlantic City is built.

Of course, the days have changed significantly since those of yore. Casinos have largely replaced the beachside amusements and oddities that once dotted the famous two-mile stretch. But still, it is no surprise that today the boardwalk hosts more of Atlantic City's attractions than any other part of town. If you stay and play on the boardwalk, you are in the middle of all the action.

The resorts described here have the major advantage of having direct boardwalk and beach access. In addition, many of the resorts are interconnected in such a way that you can explore them without ever setting foot outside. Bally's Atlantic City, Caesars, Claridge, and The Sands can all be accessed from each other via a series of overpasses.

If the resorts are not connected, however, you can still resort-hop without having to walk 2 miles down the boardwalk (or take a cab to the marina district – more on that later). There is an Atlantic City Jitney that drives from resort to resort for a nominal charge – it is transportation for tourists.

Monopolizing Monopoly

As you walk down the boardwalk, you may pass Park Place. You may pass Baltic Avenue, Pennsylvania Avenue, and North Carolina Avenue. Atlantic City really milks Parker Brothers' Monopoly game – you can buy numerous Monopoly souvenirs at most of the gift shops, and many of the signposts along the way have large Monopoly pieces inscribed with interesting historical facts.

Walking the Boardwalk

If you have the time (and the energy), then walking from the southern tip of the boardwalk to the northern tip can be fun and challenging. The resort-hotels are located on about a 2 mile stretch at the northern end, but if you walk north beyond the Showboat, the boardwalk kind of dwindles off into a regular sidewalk that brings you back into the city.

On the southern end, far away from the resorts, you are sure to see locals getting their exercise by jogging along, as you admire the expensive houses and the seemingly infinite ocean. The boardwalk ends suddenly. There is not much to see in either direction, but it can be self-fulfilling. The total walk from tip to tip is roughly 5 miles. Give yourself the afternoon, and expect to take a taxicab back.

One rainy spring afternoon, out of sheer curiosity, I was fortunate enough to walk all the way to the southern tip of the boardwalk. At around the city of Margate (2 cities south of Atlantic City, about 4 miles from the Hilton) the boardwalk stopped. There were no impressive resort-hotels or business centers or pier amusement parks, just sand and houses. It was nice, but nothing remotely similar to the bustle of Atlantic City (I could still barely make out the resort-hotels way in the distance). Moral of the story: you can't walk all the way down to Key West on the Atlantic City boardwalk. But wouldn't it be cool if you could?

If you are traveling between boardwalk resorts by car, there are two main roads parallel to the boardwalk that will connect drivers to the casinos: Atlantic Avenue and Pacific Avenue. The road closest to the Atlantic Ocean is, ironically, Pacific Avenue. Pacific Avenue separates many of the resorts from their respective self-park facilities. If you follow Pacific Avenue either up or down, you will go under many different walkways that connect these self-park lots to the resort. This is another way the resorts try to keep you inside their facilities.

Though the southern tip of the resort area is the Hilton, Atlantic City's boardwalk actually stretches for several miles south beyond that. But there are no resorts here; just private homes and apartments. Some of them are actually quite nice and they all have great views of the Atlantic Ocean.

ATLANTIC CITY HILTON

Boston Ave & The Boardwalk
Atlantic City, NJ
(609) 347-7111

The southernmost resort on the boardwalk, at the very end of the resort area, is the Atlantic City Hilton, beyond which are private residences. It is the last of the major tourist spots, as south of this the classical Jersey Shore resumes, with beach-themed shops and quaint motels and summer vacation rentals.

The Atlantic City Hilton has changed names and ownership several times over the years. The site was originally a small motel bought by Las Vegas Golden Nugget casino mogul Steve Wynn in the early 1980s. In no time it was turned into the Atlantic City Golden Nugget and was an instant and overwhelming success. But Wynn was not happy with the strict rules of Atlantic City gambling, so he decided to sell the property to Bally's/Caesars and it was renamed Bally's Grand. When Caesars Entertainment started franchising Hilton hotels, it was renamed the Atlantic City Hilton.

ARRIVING AT THE HOTEL

Since the Atlantic City Hilton is the farthest resort south, you must turn right immediately after exiting the Atlantic City Expressway. The VIP entrance to the hotel is via an underpass. Before you enter the resort's property, you will be surrounded by flat, open parking lots that seem out of place, compared to the Hilton's parking lot, an enormous multi-level structure capable of holding many times more vehicles than the independent lots. It is also considerably cheaper than they are.

As you pull into the underpass, you will be greeted with a large marble entrance fountain. Man-made fountains like this have become a staple for resort hotels, not just in Atlantic City, but also all over the country. The valet parking area is located just off the main hotel lobby.

ACCOMMODATIONS

The Atlantic City Hilton received a 4-star diamond rating from AAA, which is a very rare honor to bestow upon an Atlantic City resort (most other resorts are 3-star diamond). This is because the rooms here are somewhat larger and nicer, with more amenities than is to be expected from the other resorts. In addition, numerous levels of suites are available.

EATING AND DRINKING

The Atlantic City Hilton slightly surpasses most of the other resorts in the area when it comes to dining experiences. Like its sister resorts, Caesars and Bally's, the Hilton offers three basic levels of dining: Fine, Casual, and Bar/Lounge. And, as with the sister resorts, most eateries are in the same immediate area of the resort, one floor above the casino. However, the variety at the Hilton gives much more choice than at either Caesars or Bally's.

At the very top of the list is **Peregrines'**, which specializes in award-winning seafood dishes. It even has a 5-star rating awarded by the *American Academy of Restaurant & Hospitality Sciences*. If you like your beef, then the Atlantic City Hilton offers **The Oaks Steakhouse**. This is really a beautiful restaurant, with a comfortably dark ambiance with fine dark oak walls and an oak tree at the entrance. (Fake? Maybe.)

For Italian food, **Caruso's** offers traditional pasta entrees and a nice selection of wine. A Sunday brunch is also offered. If Asian cuisine is your preference, the **Empress Garden** serves Hunan, Szechwan, and Cantonese cuisine, and a great view of the Atlantic Ocean. In the morning, it is home to the **Empress Breakfast Buffet**.

The Atlantic City Hilton also has what every resort should have – a buffet. The **Island BBQ Buffet** has all the fare you'd expect from an Atlantic City buffet, from shrimp and crab to chicken and ribs, with a rotating menu. Also, it is one of the cheaper on-resort buffets in the area, with weekday dinner specials starting at around $17.

For the lightest fare or quick eats, **Horizons** is open 24 hours for coffee and smaller meals, whereas **Cappuccino's** offers soups and sandwiches (as well as, of course, cappuccino).

Capitalizing on the new wave of Atlantic City beach bars, the **Hilton Beach Bar** is located on the beach, accessible from the boardwalk via a sandy ramp. Much more than a standard beach bar, however, Hilton's offers personal massages as you relax in one of their several gazebos. Also play beach volleyball or horseshoes (book in advance!) or listen to a free outdoor concert. You can even swim! If you prefer to have a drink inside, the **Dizzy Dolphin** is open year-round and overlooks the boardwalk and beach.

SHOPPING AND ENTERTAINMENT

The Atlantic City Hilton suffers a bit when it comes to shopping and entertainment choices. There is one major on-site venue that is usually referred to as **The Theater at the Hilton**, but it doesn't really have a name.

The Hilton Beach Bar has various free events and performers on a much smaller scale. The **Emporium** has standard sundries; cosmetics, snacks and such (as well as various gift ideas). For upscale clothing choices, there is **Le Salon**. These are the two major retail shops at the Hilton.

On the other hand, the Atlantic City Hilton has exceptional pool and health spa facilities. The pool is indoors (open year-round), and provides an outdoor sundeck with glass walls and ceiling for added light and ambience. There is also a significant fitness and spa center for both men and women, and extensive massage options if you really want to pamper yourself. If you are having a bad hair day, **Bellezza – the Salon at Hilton** will turn it into a good one.

Conclusion

The Hilton's remote, southernmost location can be detractive to its appeal. Even the Marina District's resorts are more accessible, since you have to be in a car to get to the marina district anyway; but it is much harder and more inconvenient to walk to the Hilton. There is considerably less to see and do, and by the time you've reached it, you're pretty much out of the resort section of town.

However, this does not mean the Hilton is not a quality resort. It was the only hotel (until recently) to achieve a 4-star diamond AAA rating because of the unusually large, quality rooms and suites. In fact, though, all of the resorts in this area are quality and a traveler would be satisfied to stay in any one of them. However, since we are talking about a resort *area*, and not just a particular resort, we must focus on where it is in relation to everything else.

The higher AAA rating may draw people to the Atlantic City Hilton. However, unlike other resorts that are centered on gambling, there is no special theme here; it is a Hilton hotel with an attached casino. Take that to mean anything you want.

Tropicana Casino & Resort

Brighton & Boardwalk
Atlantic City, NJ
(609) 340-4000

The Aztar Corporation, which also owns a few other casinos, currently owns the Tropicana both in Atlantic City and Las Vegas. At the beginning, however, the Ramada Corporation announced it was purchasing the Tropicana in Las Vegas, and would build a Tropicana in Atlantic City on the site of the old Ambassador Hotel. It officially opened in late November 1981.

The Tropicana was also the first hotel to attempt a duplication of the "family friendly" atmosphere that various Las Vegas resorts have attempted. The indoor Atlantic City-themed amusement park was unsuccessful, and it was ultimately destroyed to make room for more gaming space in 1996.

Today the Tropicana is trying to give some re-birth to their more family-friendly ideals of yore. They have just added (and are continuing to add) entire facilities dedicated to non-gambling enjoyment. Expect lots of new shops and entertainment opportunities at Tropicana.

Arriving at the Hotel

When traveling down the Atlantic City Expressway, Tropicana is one of the first resort-hotels you will see, and at a glance it appears to be one of the largest; a cluster of buildings and parking lots near the southern end of the strip. Tropicana has been growing in size and quality for the past several years. It has expanded to include some new accommodations, new shopping and entertainment facilities, and much more.

Tropicana's nicest entrance is facing the boardwalk (and is meant for pedestrian traffic) so there is really no need to arrive by car. The hotel lobby is clean and pleasant, but small and not as impressive as some of the other resorts (such as the lobby of Caesars).

The resort itself has a perpetual birthday party atmosphere, some locations almost with circus birthday flair. It is one of the friendliest-looking casinos-resorts overall, with a kind of tacky classiness of the same (but slightly more subdued) caliber than The Sands.

ACCOMMODATIONS

The rooms at Tropicana are divided into several different towers. The new and more expensive Havana Tower is closet to The Quarter. Tropicana offers several different levels of suites, select ones of which can actually be booked online (unlike most other resorts, where you must call to make reservations for rooms other than standard sizes). The rooms are located in several different towers.

Tropicana is one of the only resorts in Atlantic City with both an indoor and outdoor pool; though both pools are rather small. Tropicana has a complete health club and spa facility, including massages, a Jacuzzi and sauna, as well as various pieces of fitness equipment. The pool and spa area is small in general, so if you're looking for a resort with a large pool or spa, Tropicana will not satisfy your needs. However, there is so much else to do at this resort that there may not even be time for a swim.

WHAT TO DO AT THE TROP

The Tropicana really shines when it comes to the eclectic and vast selection of dining, shopping and entertainment choices. There are some famous chains as well as Tropicana exclusives.

There are basically three entertainment sections within the resort. There's **The MarketPlace**, which consists mostly of inexpensive fast foods and a few gift stands, the more established **Main** section, which has nearly all gambling choices (although The MarketPlace has a few slots) and some fine dining choices. Finally, the newest addition, **The Quarter** is a top-notch mall and entertainment facility. All facilities within Tropicana are easily accessible from each other.

Since the opening of The Quarter, many of the food and shopping establishments have been shuffled around. So don't be surprised if your favorite shop is in the MarketPlace one day, and in The Quarter the next day.

MAIN SECTION

If you want a more upscale dinner that doesn't involve navigating the MarketPlace, **Verdi** is a good choice. Located immediately off the casino floor, Verdi's is one of the nicest Restaurants at Tropicana, and specializes in a wide variety of top-of-the-line choices in a sophisticated, white tablecloth-type setting. Tropicana offers other fine dining choices as well, including **Wellington's Steak and Seafood** and **Golden Dynasty** for top-of-the-line Asian cuisine.

In the middle of the casino action is **Tiffany Lounge** (you'll recognize it as there is a huge indoor tree in the middle of the casino's largest atrium), which is home to lots of rotating talent and bands. Plus, some casino events may require that participants gather around the lounge; so at times it gets very crowded.

And then there's **Top of the Trop** – a small bar and lounge located on the very top of the Tropicana. At any time, Top of the Trop offers probably the best view of the Atlantic City Skyline from on land. Since the Tropicana is one of the southernmost resorts, just look north and see all the glitzy resorts; even the Marina district! At night, there are frequent lounge performances (singers and musicians) and on a clear day the view is incredible.

Entertainment venues at Tropicana (featuring performances of some kind) are dispersed across the complex. The main venue is the **Tropicana Showroom**, Tropicana's large-scale event center. Tickets are required for most events and are available at the box office. Smaller venues around the resort are generally free and much more intimate. **Top of the Trop**, **Corky's Ribs & BBQ**, and **Tiffany Lounge** all have live acts throughout the day.

If you like Comedy, **The Comedy Stop at Tropicana** is one of the older comedy clubs in Atlantic City (it opened in 1983). There is a constantly rotating collection of both headliners and local comics. Entry to this club requires tickets purchased either at the door or in advance.

THE MARKETPLACE

Before The Quarter, one of Tropicana's greatest features was **The MarketPlace**, a great selection of shops, restaurants and entertainment. This is part of Tropicana's large expansion that culminates with the opening of The Quarter; a major entertainment and shopping experience (discussed in the next section).

The Marketplace is basically a small shopping center and food court that is contained both within the Tropicana itself and outside, along the boardwalk. With the exception of **Hooters**, this is a family-friendly area. There are all sorts of shops and eateries around The MarketPlace; there is even a bandstand in the central area, so you don't have to be in a casino or bar to listen to live music!

These are generally casual places with laid-back ambience and generally inexpensive fare. Among the choices are **Corky's Ribs & BBQ** (which offers live music from time to time), **Adam Good Deli** (1 of 2 in the resort), and **Boardwalk Favorites**. If you need to eat and eat and eat some more, then the **Beachfront Buffet** is located just off the MarketPlace.

For just drinks and lounging around, there are some nice choices. **Firewaters** has a huge selection of beer – 101 according to their website. It is a bar; not terribly comfortable, but if you like beer in all its manifestations, you'll be at home!

THE QUARTER

On par with the latest in ever-expanding shopping and entertainment facilities, the newest major overhaul of the Tropicana is **The Quarter**. With a grand opening which occurred late Fall 2004, this attraction is a major step-up for any Atlantic City resort; finally resort owners are attempting once again to draw a family crowd to Atlantic City. This newest non-gambling attraction has been compared to The Forum Shops at Caesars Palace in Las Vegas. Tropicana hopes that their attraction will do for Atlantic City what The Forum Shops did for Las Vegas.

The Tropicana has experimented with family-themed areas in the past, namely an indoor family amusement park (part of the former TropWorld). Unfortunately the attempt failed and it has been primarily a gambling-oriented resort. Hopefully, The Quarter will usher in a new era of entertainment for the area. Other resorts are doing similar things, and even some off-boardwalk properties are catering more to the family crowd than before, but at this point Tropicana is taking the largest step.

What is The Quarter? It is a shopping, dining, and entertainment facility that features a plethora of different activities for everybody. Modeled after the resorts of Old Havana, Cuba (pre-Castro), there are shops, restaurants, shows, and more! Stepping through the gateway into this heavily-themed mall is reminiscent of the Forum Shops in Las Vegas, though on a smaller scale. The ceiling is domed, painted with clouds, and the indoor "streets" and facades of the shops offer a sense of perpetual Cuban dusk.

Among the facilities: Tropicana has Atlantic City's first and only **IMAX** Theater. Additionally, there are several nightclub and lounge areas, such as **Cuba Libre** and **The Sound of Philadelphia**. **Houdini's Magic Shop**, a classic in Las Vegas, is finally making its way to Atlantic City at Tropicana. Also enjoy browsing the classic American Midwest style at **The Old Farmer's Almanac General Store**. If you want some cool sleuth gadgets, definitely check out **The Spy Store**, which has an array of great consumer spy equipment for the exceptionally paranoid consumer. Of course, there are also some great upscale clothing and jewelry stores, such as **Erwin Pearl** and **Chico's** and even **Brooks Brothers**.

There is and will be much more to see and do at The Quarter, since it is a brand new facility it will probably be expanding for a while, so who knows what the future will bring! For an aesthetically enjoyable and creative shopping and entertainment experience, Tropicana's The Quarter would make Las Vegas resorts proud.

CONCLUSION

The Tropicana is a great choice for families or people wishing to do more than just gamble. Despite its somewhat southerly and out-of-the-way location, there is much to do here! It has larger facilities and is very colorful and upbeat. The Quarter is the most unique shopping experience in Atlantic City, and it has a much friendlier atmosphere than other resorts, where the principle diversion is gambling. Though the casino floor here is large, there is much more to the Tropicana than meets the gambler's eye.

It is also one of the two closest resorts to the boardwalk Convention Hall, so if you want to be as close as possible to Miss America, you can't do much better than this.

TRUMP PLAZA

Mississippi Ave. & Boardwalk
Atlantic City, NJ
(609) 441-6000

You must hand it to Donald Trump – this man has an aura that is unlike any other real estate tycoon (rich and famous and broke and married and divorced and rich again and host of a successful television show). He has truly done his homework. He is an entrepreneur and a take-charge kind of guy. His company owns three resort-hotels in Atlantic City, not to mention numerous other properties all over the place. He is partially responsible for legalizing gambling in Atlantic City. But most of all, he keeps his name on our lips.

Recently, however, Donald Trump's Atlantic City Resorts have hit some financial trouble. When the Borgata opened in summer 2003, these resorts were hit especially hard. In fact, the following summer, the three Trump resorts in Atlantic City filed Chapter 11 bankruptcy (a move which the corporation called "restructuring").

Still, they are among the premier resorts in Atlantic City, and – for those familiar with The Donald's "style", you will definitely feel at home here. Trump Plaza has gone though several legs of history (you can still see remnants of the old "Trump World's Fair" casino façade inside Boardwalk Hall if you look hard enough), and the resort is also Donald Trump's first casino in Atlantic City.

Trump Plaza is actually a combination of one large resort casino and one much smaller casino. The smaller one was initially owned by

Playboy Enterprises, but the resort did very poorly, and Trump purchased the resort and added it to his Trump Plaza complex, first as a regular resort and finally, in 1996, as a casino.

Arriving at the Hotel

Located just south of Caesars, Trump Plaza has among the best locations in Atlantic City. In fact, when driving and exiting the Atlantic City Expressway, Trump Plaza is literally right in your face. The most prominent landmark is the Trump Plaza self-parking lot. Directly in front of it is a large, ultra-bright motion screen (reminiscent of the many on Times Square) that advertises whatever offers or promotions the Trump Plaza is offering at the time. Below the sign is a fountain – cute visual eye-candy that does not really match the bright parking garage behind it

Self-parking is closest, but if you want the VIP valet experience, you can drive underneath the Trump Plaza entrance. The valet entrance is not as impressive as Caesars right next door, so you really don't need to drive in for the best possible experience.

When you first enter Trump Plaza, the inherent Trump-ed-ness is immediately apparent. For one thing, the walls and props in the resort all glisten almost too brightly, and everything is coated with shiny golden paneling. The idea may be for the place to look rich, but the Trump décor is overstated.

Accommodations

It is evident that Trump Plaza (as well as the other Trump casinos) caters towards the big-budget gambler. In this manner, the suites offered are slightly better than suites at resorts designed with the more casual gambler in mind. The check-in area is located under the casino just inside the valet parking / main entrance. Shiny chandeliers adorn the ceiling and the nearby escalator leads immediately up to the casino floor.

The resort is a bit shy of eight hundred regular rooms, and additionally about one hundred forty suites of various shapes and sizes. As with many casino-resorts, on weekends these suites are reserved; so if you want to enjoy one, either gamble or travel during a weekday.

Eating and Drinking

Trump Plaza's restaurants and lounges are of the standard fare in Atlantic City. The resort has exactly what you would expect; a tried-and-true formula for fine dining, casual dining, and lounges. As you'll notice, the finer restaurants are located in a special dining area on the sixth floor of the resort, while the casual restaurants and lounges are somewhat more scattered about.

If you're looking for high-quality Italian food, your best bet is definitely **Roberto's Ristorante**, located on the sixth floor of the resort. While decidedly overpriced, it offers standard Italian food with upscale ambience. It is one of the better-situated restaurants in the resort; it overlooks the Atlantic Ocean so you can long to be on the beach while you eat. For a more extensive wine list in a contemporary setting, there is also **EVO**, with more inexpensive prices and a wide range of cocktails.

On the other hand, if steak is more your thing, check out **Max's Steakhouse**. Vegetarians Beware: there is little besides meat on this carnivorous menu. This is also located on the sixth floor. Or, if you prefer Asian food, **Fortunes** is a class act all the way with Cantonese, Mandarin, and Szechwan menu choices. For Asian food in a more casual setting, Trump Plaza is also host to **China Café**, which features a well-appointed Sushi bar.

But fine dining is not the only option. **Broadway Buffet**, which is located below the casino, is Trump Plaza's signature buffet. There is also a new **Rainforest Café** with a lovely entrance directly off the boardwalk, and the same ambiance and fare you'd expect from the chain. **New Yorker** is the 24-hour on-premises eatery located on the main lobby level of the resort. Since Trump is known for real estate development in the Big Apple, all of his resorts have a restaurant dedicated to a New York theme.

The Beach Bar at Trump Plaza, open in the summertime, is Trump's only beach bar (in the recent Atlantic City beach bar tradition). It is located across the boardwalk directly on the beach. Access is via a sandy wooden walkway. The Beach Bar features live music on occasion. Finally, **Boardwalker Bar** is located just inside off the boardwalk, and is a smallish quaint place for a drink. And there is also a **Starbucks**.

SHOPPING AND ENTERTAINMENT

Trump Plaza is home to the Plaza Showroom, a semi-large venue (by Atlantic City standards). Tickets are required for events here, which sometimes feature various Broadway shows on tour and topical performances on occasion. If you want some free live music, be sure to catch a live musical performance at **The Beach Bar**, where you can stick around as long as you're drinking. Trump Plaza may also, on occasion, sponsor an event at the nearby Boardwalk Convention Hall, in the **Adrian Phillips Ballroom**.

There are a limited number of shopping possibilities on the premises. **The Front Page Gift Shop** is a standard gift and sundries supply store, which is open 24 hours a day. **Cache**, a popular chain in Atlantic City resorts, is an upscale women's fashion store. **BARRON for her** sells designer handbags. Trump Plaza does not have the variety of shopping and entertainment opportunities that most other resorts in midtown do (such as Bally's and Caesars). However, due to its very close proximity to many other off-site features, it almost doesn't matter that this resort lacks these amenities.

POOL AND RECREATIONAL FACILITIES

The seventh floor of Trump Plaza houses the pool and spa facilities. There is a charge to use these facilities (even for hotel guests) but it is a nice area, and decently-equipped.

The **Plaza Spa** offers several choices for relaxation and spa treatment options, such as Jacuzzis, steam rooms, and saunas. Swedish and Aromatherapy massages and various body treatments are available for an extra charge. Reservations should be made in advance. Tanning beds are also available for an additional charge, as well as a small fitness facility with all the standard workout and cardio equipment expected of a small gym.

In addition to the indoor features, there is an outside recreation facility that has two tennis courts and even shuffleboard (rental fees apply to space, tennis balls available for purchase). The pool, Olympic-size, is one of the largest in Atlantic City. Unlike the other spa facilities, the pool is free to use for hotel guests.

CONCLUSION

Trump Plaza is small; there are few rooms and not a lot of on-property entertainment options other than the large gambling floor. However, its proximity to many more attractions on the boardwalk (both in and out of the resorts) makes Trump Plaza an ideal choice if you prefer a smaller hotel. It promises an upscale atmosphere about it and clearly likes to think it is of high quality; which it probably was, ten years ago.

CAESARS ATLANTIC CITY

2100 Pacific Avenue
Atlantic City, NJ
(609) 348-4411

Caesars Atlantic City was only the second casino to establish itself in Atlantic City, opening in 1979 as Caesars Boardwalk Regency. Although it boasts over 1,200 rooms in four different towers, the resort is still organized and manageable. And unlike many of the other resorts along the boardwalk, Caesars Atlantic City has maintained consistent ownership of the property, enabling its emergence as one of the best-known and most constant landmarks on the boardwalk.

Contrary to popular belief, Caesars Atlantic City is not also known as Caesars Palace. Caesars Palace is the Caesars Entertainment company's flagship resort in Las Vegas. In addition to Caesars Atlantic City and Caesars Palace, Caesars Entertainment also owns and operates many other gaming properties all over the world, including the Atlantic City Hilton, Bally's Park Place, and other Las Vegas venues. This makes the Caesars Connection Card a good choice for gamblers – some benefits are applicable to a large number of establishments.

ARRIVING AT THE HOTEL

The easiest way to arrive at Caesars is probably by car. The VIP parking option is inexpensive and very convenient (about $4 will buy you either valet or self-parking). Arriving this way will also allow you to see one of the only sites in Caesars that emulates its incomparable Las Vegas counterpart. The main entrance features a majestic horse-drawn chariot and grand Roman columns that appear to hold up the entire entrance. The main entrance is much smaller than it appears on postcards and is in fact a very cleverly built façade.

As you enter the hotel, you will immediately see an escalator leading up to the lobby and a huge casino right behind it. But don't go into the casino just yet – the Caesars main hotel lobby on the next level is one of the best in Atlantic City.

On entrance to the lobby it appears that one has stepped into the cool twilight of a Roman evening. The dusky ambient lighting evokes a sense of peaceful calm, highlighting a pale blue vaulted ceiling painted with wispy white clouds. Artificial torches line the second floor balconies and scattered oases of palm trees complete the scene.

Look up as you ascend the escalator, and you will see large Roman statues above. When you arrive at the top, the **Temple Bar** – a dining establishment - in one corner surrounded by columns is an ideal place to sit and enjoy a drink. Finally, in the far corner, the statue of Augustus Caesar stands proudly atop an indoor fountain. This is the trademark of Caesars Entertainment, informing you that yes, you have entered Ancient Rome.

ACCOMMODATIONS

In general, Caesars caters to a somewhat wealthier crowd. If you are a high roller and/or are staying in one of their many luxury suites, you have additional amenities not available to those staying in regular rooms, including VIP check-in and use of the Augustus Club. Suites here come in many shapes and sizes, with some exceeding 1,000 square feet. Expect to pay excessively in some way for these high-class rooms.

The check-in desk is in the hotel lobby, on the left when you reach the top of the escalator. If you are in a suite, however, you may take advantage of the VIP check-in on the other side of the lobby. Caesars Atlantic City used to be – but is not any more - one of the larger resort-hotels in the area. The 1,200 rooms are divided into four different "towers": North and South Temple Towers, the Ocean Tower, and the Centurion Tower. The North and South Towers, accessible immediately off the hotel lobby, make up the original hotel before the expansion several years back.

Short of choosing your room type, you generally cannot choose the tower you will stay in; all four towers have varying levels of accommodation. If you can, stay in the Ocean or Centurion Towers – the North and South Towers look a bit older and worn - though the rooms themselves are still quality, many of the hallways and public areas have seen quite a bit of wear and tear.

Overall, Caesars Atlantic City has one of the best locations on the boardwalk. It is almost the geographic center of the resort area, and is generally located on one of the busiest sections of the boardwalk. Staying at Caesars means staying near most of the city's attractions.

Rooms Overlooking the Lobby

Although you can't "officially" choose your room and the Temple Towers are the two oldest towers of Caesars Atlantic City, if you're lucky, you may get one of the Temple Tower rooms overlooking the hotel lobby. Its perpetual evening glow will soothe you to sleep. The only downside – you can't tell the time of day by looking out your window.

If you are interested in staying at Caesars Atlantic City, your best bet is to call the resort directly or visit its website online. If you call directly you generally get the best deals and availability information. Also, keep in mind that summer weekends are by far the busiest and most expensive. After all, Atlantic City is, above all else, a beach resort.

SHOPPING AND ACTIVITIES

Caesars offers several on-property shopping experiences, most of which are located past the main lobby. The casino itself is split into two floors (the non-smoking floor is significantly smaller, and located on the lobby level). Most locations in the resort converge on this central location, with escalators that will take you up to third floor dining or down to the main casino floor.

The shops within the hotel are generally small but packed with merchandise that is (1) expensive and branded with the Caesars logo, (2) expensive jewelry and clothing, or (3) expensive sundries. It's fun to look around for a while, but, again, don't expect this shopping experience to be like The Forum Shops at Caesars Palace.

Caesars Exclusively sells mostly branded merchandise. You will also find **Brandeis Jewelers**, **Andrew Geller**, **Landau Jewelers**, and **Bellezza – the Salon at Caesars**. **Emperor's Essentials** is located just off the main lobby, as you exit the resort to the self-park garage (it is designed for last-minute impulse gifts).

If you're looking for some pampering, the Ocean Tower houses **The Spa at Caesars**, which features an outdoor swimming pool (open in the summertime only), fitness equipment, and other full-service spa treatments. The spa is accessible to all guests, but keep in mind that if you are not staying in the Ocean Tower, you will have to make the trip down, through the lobby, and back up again.

Caesars Atlantic City is also home to the **Circus Maximus Theatre**, which can seat up to 1,100 people (almost as many as the hotel itself can accommodate). This is a major entertainment venue, with performances of all kinds – musical, comedy, even Las Vegas-style revues. You can buy your tickets directly from the box office or from an online ticket vendor (depending on the performance). The theater is located directly off the central escalators (where the shops are located).

Some events are held in the smaller **Palladium Ballroom**, which can be altered to accommodate many different events. If you are in the mood for a smaller setting, Caesars has numerous smaller venues with ongoing performances nightly. Walk or ride the escalator downstairs from the Circus Maximus Theatre entrance, and you will find yourself right in the middle of **The Party Pit**. It's a section on the main casino floor with the Toga Bar, which features plasma TVs, a small dance floor, and a small stage.

Even if you don't gamble, sitting at the bar in The Party Pit can be lots of fun. Be warned, though – this area of the casino can get crowded and loud if a band is playing. Plus, if you're not here to gamble, you may not want to be around so many people who are. In any case, if it's too much commotion, nearby is an exit to the boardwalk.

But even outside you're not at a loss for entertainment. Walk straight out from the casino and onto a walkway towards the beach. In

Atlantic City: Beyond Gambling   71

no time you will have entered an amazing little outdoor area called the
Sand Box Beach Bar. The Sand Box Beach Bar is an intimate and enjoyable setting, situated directly on the beach. What's more, if you're a VIP guest (a.k.a. a highroller or staying in a suite) then you have access to private lounge chairs facing the ocean. You're still a few hundred feet from the water's edge, but the view is spectacular. Sit back and enjoy your surroundings. The waitstaff, dressed in exotic (and revealing) swimwear, serve tropical mixed drinks, and a live band plays on the outdoor stage. Please note however, that the Sand Box Beach Bar is understandably open only in the summertime.

THE PIER AT CAESARS

On the boardwalk, directly across from Caesars Atlantic City, used to be "The Shops at Ocean One Mall" a shopping and entertainment complex. It is the southernmost pier in Atlantic City and has been inaccessible to tourists since 2002, due to its large-scale renovation. When the pier re-opens, it will be called The Pier at Caesars and will feature a host of activities, including shopping, entertainment, and even a large-scale show. The same group responsible for The Forum Shops at Caesars Palace is designing the new Pier.

The Pier has always been an entertainment and shopping venue. Its first incarnation was as the Million Dollar Pier, built in 1906. For its time, the pier was massive, and almost always crowded with entertainment, from performers such as Harry Houdini to early Miss America pageants to stumping politicians to all kinds of exhibits. The Million Dollar Pier was destroyed by fire in 1912, and has undergone multiple resurrections since.

As of this writing, The Pier at Caesars is nothing more than a steel shell, with slow progress. The expected date of opening has been pushed back several times, and it now appears that the new facility will not re-open until at least 2006. When it does open, though, I expect it shall rival Tropicana's new Quarter facility as a major non-gambling destination in the city.

DINING

Hungry? Caesars Atlantic City offers many dining options, from casual buffet to formal black-tie sit-down. On the property are several dining facilities and bars (in addition to the free alcohol available on the casino floor). Most of the eateries are located on the third floor (accessible via escalator or elevator outside the Circus Maximus Theatre).

> **Romantic Drinks**
>
> Every hotel has a romantic spot to share with your special someone. Tropicana has the most romantic bar in the city, but Caesars Forum Lounge comes close – if you plan it right. The bar is hidden from the rest of the hotel - there is a special private staircase that caters only to the lounge and the ultra-fancy Bacchanal restaurant.
>
> Go during the late evening to avoid crowds, and claim a comfy couch by the huge floor-to-ceiling windows overlooking the boardwalk and ocean. Enjoy a modestly priced drink with your lover and indulge in each other's company in the cozy and romantically-lit lounge.

When you reach the third floor, several restaurants will surround you. Many of them may be closed however; the hours of the restaurants tend to be overlapped so that not all of them are open all the time. The buffet **La Piazza** may be open for breakfast, **The Gladiator Grille** may be open for lunch, and the more upscale **Primavera** will be open for dinner. All offer basically the same quality of food, but the menu selection varies.

The quality of food may not be a major drawing point for Atlantic City but there are a lot of dining choices, particularly here at Caesars. For the most exclusive taste, head over to The **Bacchanal** restaurant and enjoy the best food that Caesars Atlantic City has to offer.

The Temple Bar in the hotel lobby has the best location and the prettiest ambience, but the hours are so limited that you really have to plan ahead if you wish to dine there. **Café Roma**, overlooking the boardwalk and ocean, is the only dining establishment in the hotel that is open 24 hours, and the food is not that spectacular. Of course, you can order food from your room, but expect high prices and low quality. If you're into gambling, Caesars loves to give out free meals to dedicated players. However, this tends to make the food somewhat overpriced for those who choose not to spend hours in the casino.

For good old-fashioned over-priced tourist fare, Caesars also boasts Atlantic City's **Planet Hollywood** restaurant. Enter from the boardwalk or from The Party Pit on the main casino floor, and treat yourself to the movie-themed decor and the exact same menu you'll find at nearly every other Planet Hollywood in the world.

CONCLUSION

Caesars started small, but it has grown. With the new Pier, it appears to be growing still. But other than the very impressive hotel lobby and a few select places within the resort, Caesars Atlantic City has less non-gambling attractions, without a lot of the bells and whistles that can be found in other resorts in the area. Caesars caters almost exclusively to its dedicated players and highrollers, making it a great place for wealthier patrons. Ordinary folk may have a harder time with the service, staff and prices, all of which may at times seem unfriendly. However, with the recent opening of the Borgata, Caesars may no longer be top pick for the ultra-elite.

If you do nothing else in Caesars Atlantic City, visit the lobby and the hotel's main entrance, if only for a few moments to experience the ambiance. My advice: walk into Caesars and bask in the glory of the lobby, then walk straight through to the overpass connecting it to the Wild Wild West Casino next door.

BALLY'S ATLANTIC CITY

Park Place & Boardwalk
Atlantic City, NJ
(609) 340-2000

If you'll notice from the address above, Bally's Atlantic City has perhaps the most prestigious, well-known address in Atlantic City. Even people who have never been to Atlantic City will recognize the name of this intersection. (HINT: Its just before you pass GO and collect $200.)

Bally's is actually comprised of three separate resort-hotel-casino areas, which makes it collectively one of the largest resorts in Atlantic City. Bally's Wild Wild West Casino, Bally's Park Place (the "main resort"), and Claridge Casino have combined casino floor areas of eighty thousand square feet! Two of the three areas have hotel rooms available – Bally's Atlantic City and the Claridge Tower - adding up to over two thousand rooms in the complex with two different fitness/spa/pool areas.

All three resort areas are located side-by-side along the boardwalk, with Bally's Wild Wild West Casino at the southern end, Claridge Casino at the north and Bally's Park Place in between. Right next door is Caesars Atlantic City, which is owned by the same company that owns Bally's Atlantic City, Caesars Entertainment. However, Caesars and Bally's are decidedly separate, connected only by a walkway on the southern end of Bally's Wild Wild West Casino.

Bally's Park Place, the original resort of the Bally's complex, was the third resort in Atlantic City. Many years later, Park Place Entertainment (now Caesars Entertainment) built The Wild Wild West Casino next door, and ultimately acquired the Claridge to the north.

The resort is huge; because of this, more buses go from New York City directly to Bally's than to any other casino in Atlantic City. Luckily, Bally's Atlantic City is located right in the middle of the boardwalk, with easy access to many of the surrounding casinos. It is also right across from the Atlantic City Outlets and near the bus terminal, making it an all-around ideal location. Of course, in addition to gaming, all three of these facilities have great restaurant and shopping possibilities.

Bally's Wild Wild West Casino

Only in a casino resort town can you go from Ancient Rome to the old American West in just a few steps. Bally's Wild Wild West is immediately adjacent to Caesars Atlantic City – which is no surprise, since the same company owns them both.

Completed in 1997, Bally's Wild Wild West Casino is perhaps the most themed casino along the strip, a fact that's very apparent from both the boardwalk side and the street side. The exterior is designed to look like many old west buildings squished together, and the "buildings" are even painted with bright and pastel colors – just like the olden days (Wink, Wink).

This casino is perhaps the only theme-based casino you will find in Atlantic City that emulates the themes of Las Vegas hotels. The Golden Nugget on Fremont Street in downtown Las Vegas immediately came to mind when I first entered Bally's; in this case, however, Atlantic City far outshines its Nevadan counterpart.

Although Caesars' façade exists mostly in the resort's main entrance and lobby, Bally's Wild Wild West Casino goes all out – each room in this huge building is intricately decorated to resemble a western town during the gold rush; there is a waterfall, a general store, and many western-style buildings. It is designed to look like you are outside in the evening, strolling through a neighborhood of the Old West. There are even animatronic western folk that wish you good luck as you gamble or amble.

GETTING TO THE CASINO

Bally's Wild Wild West Casino is officially a part of Bally's Park Place (right next door) but it stands alone in many aspects. If you are driving, you will probably wind up driving into Bally's Park Place and parking your car with them. If you are arriving by bus (since there is no interesting main entrance, it really doesn't matter how you arrive), the bus terminal is immediately in between the regular Bally's casino and the Wild Wild West Casino. Take your pick.

There is, however, a unique pedestrian entrance that does not face the boardwalk and does not have any parking. It is probably there to entice you to visit the Wild Wild West if you initially had plans to do otherwise. When you first enter the casino from the boardwalk, you are greeted with old-fashioned saloon-style doors (though they do not swing in both directions). From there, an animatronic gold-digger (the good kind) and his trusty mule lure you inside. The whole entrance from the boardwalk is designed to look like a mountainside with a small stream. If you stick around for a few minutes you will get an animatronic show – think the Forum Shops show in Las Vegas but scaled down and with a western theme.

EXPLORING THE CASINO

Bally's Wild Wild West Casino is only a casino – there are no hotel rooms and no valet parking. There are a plethora of restaurants and a few shops, but if you intend to spend the night here, you are forced to stay at Bally's Park Place, Claridge Casino, or the casino floor. The latter choice is not recommended.

However, Bally's Wild Wild West Casino is one of the only casinos that you can really enjoy strolling through without having to gamble. Since you're on a vacation that doesn't have to revolve around gambling, the "show" that's put on makes this is a great place to visit.

The casino is divided into many different areas, though they all offer similar games and maintain a basic décor. If you start at the Caesars walkway (the farthest point south of the casino) head down the escalators and immediately enter Coyote Kate's Slot Parlor (remember: you don't have to enter from the boardwalk – these casinos are connected indoors). This is a small room consisting of just slot machines. It is one of the smaller and least-decorated rooms of the Wild Wild West, but it's still very well done.

Go Ahead... Be Cheap!

Bally's Wild Wild West Casino is one of the most inexpensive places to eat and gamble in Atlantic City. You can have a good meal for under $10 here, and there are numerous nickel slots and table games with the lowest minimum bids. In addition, the hotel rooms here are the most reasonably priced, even on weekends, and seem to be generally more available than most other resorts in the area.

If you'll notice, on the floor is a "wooden" path that leads through the parlor. This path will actually take you through the entire Wild Wild West Casino or into Bally's Park Place. This is probably the official "I'm under 21 and must not leave this here trail" path, but it provides a nice tour of the casino.

As you begin walking, if you look up, you'll see that the entire "second floor" of the casino has mini-windows, western-style balconies, and mannequin townsfolk. You'll also pass under mini-arches and by many slot machines as you make your way north.

Since the walkway from Caesars is not the main entrance to the casino, eventually you'll arrive at it by following the path. This is where the animatronic mule and prospector are – and you can catch a show every few minutes.

Keep wandering through the "town". Just beyond the main entrance, over your head, is a mini train track and a working train – it is above the Mountain Bar, which is a great place to have a drink in a western-style saloon. You will have several opportunities to exit the casino and head over to Bally's Park Place.

Although the scenery in the Wild Wild West Casino doesn't change very much, it is thorough and consistent. There are an abundance of animatronics and interesting western sights to tantalize your eyes and ears.

DINING

Bally's Wild Wild West Casino really shines when it comes to its eateries. From the casino's main entrance off the boardwalk, just past the animatronic show, you'll see the **Mountain Bar**, one of the coolest places to have a drink in Atlantic City. Although separated from the casino with nothing more than a series of posts, you really feel like you're in the Rocky Mountains, drinking suds with fellow western folk. Mountain Bar on occasion features live country music.

The bar is long (ninety feet!) and can hold over a hundred people. Plus, it is open twenty-four hours a day, so you can stroll in any time you want. There are also video slots at the bar – but why bother using them when there are so many slot machines right outside?

If you're hungry, mosey on over to the **Lone Star Snack Bar**, right next door to the Mountain Bar. Here is one of the few fast-food-type establishments located right on the casino floor, so you can eat while on the run. The fare here is more expensive than a non-resort fast food restaurant (such as those on the boardwalk) but it's nearby and the food is decent. Seating is very limited, though; so maybe stake claim to a chair while your travel buddy waits in line. No travel buddy? Eat standing up or go during the late night hours.

For quick sweets, you can get donuts, soda, or other deli-style snackables from **Gold Tooth Gerties Buns & Bagels**, which is located directly underneath the escalator connecting this casino to Caesars. Its food for fun,sometimes they even give away free samples. And through the large kitchen windows, you can also watch the doughnuts being made as you wait in line to place your order.

THE VIRGINIA CITY BUFFET

If you're really hungry, however, you may want to consider one of the best buffets in Atlantic City. Near the far north end of Bally's Wild Wild West Casino, up to the second floor via escalator, is the **Virginia City Buffet**. This buffet has a wider selection of food from any of the other buffets in the area.

The Virginia City Buffet is more secluded then the other dining and drinking opportunities of the Wild Wild West, but the décor does not stop when you ride the escalator – the room which houses the buffet is designed to looked like a western porch – the color scheme and buildings are the same, but without the noisy slots. Portions of the dining tables are located in one of several "porch" areas, while the others are located in the "outdoors" area, with lampposts lighting the way. If you are in Bally's Wild Wild West Casino, you definitely need to check out this buffet (however, you must be 21 to eat here).

The food selection is extraordinary. There are several "stations" that mimic a mini-mall of food. From John Wang's Asian cuisine to the Remember the Alamode dessert station, the tongue-in-cheek humor of Bally's is carried throughout. You can even get a full steak cooked to order. As this is "officially" (as touted by the people at Bally's) one of the best buffets in Atlantic City, it is frequently crowded. On busy weekends, expect to make a reservation up to several hours in advance.

BALLY'S WILD WILD WEST - CONCLUSION

As pure casino tackiness and themed environments go, Bally's Wild Wild West Casino is the best in Atlantic City. Approachable and not nearly as "upscale" as some of the destinations, this casino is perfect for the Jane and Joe Everyman (no relation) who may want to gamble a little bit, and also have some cute fun.

BALLY'S PARK PLACE

Bally's Park Place is the "main casino" of the Bally's complex. It is home to the large Bally's Tower where most of the resort's overnight accommodations are located, as well as The Spa at Bally's. Bally's Park Place was the original resort - Wild Wild West Casino was built in 1997 and the Claridge resort acquired in 2002.

Bally's Park Place was the third casino resort corporation in Atlantic City. In the late 1970s it bought and leveled the Marlborough-Blenheim Hotel and renovated the nearby Dennis Hotel. However, it barely surpassed the five hundred-room minimum required for a gambling license. In 1988, Bally's was the first casino to exceed one thousand rooms with the introduction of the Tower, which to this day remains one of the most contemporary-looking buildings on the boardwalk.

Since Bally's Park Place is Bally's main casino, and since Bally's Atlantic City is collectively the largest casino resort in Atlantic City, it is understandable that most of the buses, traffic, and pedestrian thoroughfare converge at Bally's. That, added to its ideal location—right in the middle of the boardwalk resort area—makes Bally's Park Place one of the most popular resorts in town.

ARRIVING AT THE HOTEL

The tall and contemporary Bally's Tower stands out immediately from the rest of the crowd. It is sleek, dark and shiny, and at night it lights up with a checkered motion lighting display. Though Bally's Park Place is a significantly bigger complex and has more hotel rooms (in the main building), the Tower itself is impressive, with a large "Bally's" sign on the top – just so you don't forget what building you're looking at.

After entering the City from the Atlantic City Expressway, make a left (head north/south), but don't go too far, as the entrance to Bally's Park Place is nearby. The self-parking lot and underpass for valet parking are in between the main resort and the Wild Wild West Casino. If you choose to self-park (or are taking a bus), then once you leave the self-park connecting walkway you can choose to go left to the main resort and check-in, or right to the West.

Valet Parking – as with many resorts – requires you to pull your car into an underpass. The decor seems almost like tacky western, but with a touch of Victorian. As you will soon see, Bally's Park Place is a mix of themes that can only be described as Bally's. If you choose valet parking, enter the main doors and immediately head up the escalator. You will be brought onto a platform right in between the main casino floor and the large check-in counter. This whole area is a single massive room; the front desk is only slightly removed by a single step up.

From the top of the escalator, you'll immediately notice the décor and ambience of Bally's Park Place; it is a combination of several different styles that seem to fuse together in a somewhat odd but understandable way. The carpet has a nature-theme to it, green and flowery, as is some of the wallpaper. However, the lighting scheme is exceptionally bright and flashy – even for a casino – and very much at odds with nature. The ceiling and walls of the hotel lobby have a shiny flashiness about them, surrounding and overlooking the "bad-tacky" artificial plants in the middle of the room.

Bally's Loves to Joke

Bally's Park Place has a sort of tongue-in-cheek humor about itself, making the environment much more relaxed and casual than a more "serious" resort. Consider the self-park lot, named "Bally's Parking Place", and their steak house, named "Prime Place".

The whole facility has an un-updated 1970s feel to it. The Las Vegas counterpart shares this unique combination of visual traits, but unfortunately, in Atlantic City some of it just comes off as old. This is one reason why, in my opinion, Bally's Wild Wild West Casino is so important to the success of Bally's Atlantic City. It shows that Bally's *intends* the look of kinda 1970s, kinda Victorian, kinda nature and kinda glitzy, and it isn't simply aging or the result of bad planning. The inclusion of Wild Wild West Casino into the Bally's experience makes this Bally's Park Place casino much more special than if either of them were to stand alone.

ACCOMMODATIONS

As is to be expected, you are offered a plethora of different kinds of rooms and suites, ranging from basic rooms to lavish suites. If you desire, there are even relatively inexpensive Jacuzzi suites available for the romantics. These suites can sometimes be booked online, depending on availability.

However, booking a room at Bally's Park Place means your room may be located in one of three different hotel areas. Bally's Tower is generally the most upscale, the main building is the most accessible and least expensive, and the Claridge Tower is the most recently renovated.

Atlantic City: Beyond Gambling   83

A note about the Claridge Tower: since Bally's added the Claridge resort to its roster of Atlantic City destinations in 2002, all Claridge rooms are now booked through the main Bally's Atlantic City reservation system. If rooms are available, you can choose to stay in Claridge if you prefer. But more often than not (particularly on busy nights) you may be assigned a room in Claridge upon check-in. Claridge Tower rooms are the furthest by a long shot from Bally's casinos, facilities, and spa (although Claridge does have amenities of its own).

EXPLORING THE RESORT

There is a major and accessible walkway that connects Bally's Park Place to the self-park garage, and finally to the Wild Wild West Casino. This walkway is also where resort guests access their rooms in Bally's main building, as well as Bally's pool and spa area. Heading north and entering the main casino floor from this walkway: to your left is the check-in area, straight ahead is the escalator from the valet parking facility, and to the right is the large casino. If you keep walking straight, you'll shortly hit the walkway that connects Bally's Park Place to Claridge next door.

Bally's Park Place is one of the easiest resorts to navigate; mostly because the main area is one huge square. And right in the middle of the casino floor is a very large, very long escalator that takes you up from the first floor to restaurants and keno and track betting rooms.

In the main lobby area (near the check-in counter on the westernmost side of the casino floor) is a gift shop and a high limit slot room. Walking further back past the front desk brings you to the elevators that take you up to Bally's Tower. In the opposite direction, walk directly through the casino floor, and you will walk out onto the boardwalk. Overall, it is a simple resort to navigate, and everything is generally within a short walking distance.

EATING AND DRINKING

Though Bally's considers its Wild Wild West Casino and Park Place casino as part of the same resort, the dining choices and experiences are decidedly different. You can generally expect a much more upscale dining experience at Park Place than at Wild Wild West. As with the other

Caesars Entertainment resorts in Atlantic City, most of the major food choices are located in a central area directly above the casino floor (take the central escalator).

Consider **Arturo's**: an upscale dining experience with a New York style setting and Italian dining (think Little Italy). The view here of the boardwalk and ocean is great, and the food selection is among the best Bally's Park Place offers. Food choices include various types of meat and fresh seafood.

Prime Place is Bally's steakhouse, and one of the best in Atlantic City, earning top honors in the *Zagat Restaurant Survey*. Prime Place also has a self-serve salad bar as well as a great view, similar to Arturo's.

For an Italian experience, try **Luna**. It is Bally's most romantic restaurant, and when weather is agreeable, you can choose to dine on their patio. They also have an extensive selection of wine – and a private dining room if you wish to hold an event.

Since Bally's Park Place is a casual and friendly resort, the selection of casual dining experiences is extensive. They have the city's only **Johnny Rockets**. Near the Baccarat Pit is **Noodles & Zen Sum**, a quick-eats Asian restaurant that attempts to emulate a sushi bar (with a cook-at-your-table-style display kitchen).

On the walkway connecting Park Place to the Wild Wild West Casino is a staircase that leads down to Bally's buffet: **The Sidewalk Café**. This is the most removed (and most hidden) restaurant at Bally's. In addition, **Gatsby's Grill & Oyster Bar** has a very unusual selection of quick foods. They serve traditional hamburgers, chowders, fresh desserts, and have a full raw bar (clams and such). For a quick and tasty bite at any time of the day, **Animations Coffee Shop** is great! It has a cartoon theme. In addition to the 24-hour operating schedule, it has a lot of choice, and you can choose to sit and eat or get your food to go.

Want only a drink? From the upscale **Blue Martini** (with live music on occasion) to the generic but ideally-situated **Lobby Lounge**, Bally's Park Place has a limited but sufficient selection of bars and lounges. In summertime, the **Bikini Beach Bar** is one of several new outdoor bars located directly on the beach. While not unique within the confines of Atlantic City, these beach bars are definitely one of the advantages Atlantic City has over Las Vegas.

SHOPPING AND ENTERTAINMENT

A fundamental flaw at Bally's Park Place is their lack of any significant venues for entertainment events. There is a Main Ballroom, which can be converted to accommodate many different kinds of events, but it is small and unsuitable for anything larger than a few hundred people. Bally's is well aware of this flaw, and touts that their "big events" are hosted at the nearby Atlantic City Boardwalk Hall.

Their availability for live music is also limited – The Blue Martini lounge has some live performances, but that is the extent of the live entertainment options at Bally's (unless you head over to the Mountain Bar in the Wild Wild West Casino, which has live country music on weekends and busy times of the year). Claridge next door has a venue that seats about 550 people, which is small considering that other venues in Atlantic City can fit 2,000 people or more.

THE SPA AT BALLY'S

One thing I believe all major resorts should have (and particularly casino resorts) is a spectacular pool and spa facility. Maybe because Atlantic City has the beach, or because it's freezing half the time, Atlantic City sorely lacks quality pool and spa facilities. The pools are generally very small, the spa and fitness areas lack sufficient equipment, and many resorts charge admission to their facilities (even for hotel guests!).

I mention this because **The Spa at Bally's** is one of the best pool and spa facilities in Atlantic City. Until the Borgata opened, it was the undisputed king of Atlantic City resort spas. This is not to say that it is remotely comparable to the extravagant multi-acre facilities in Las Vegas, but if having a good spa facility is integral to your vacation experience, then there is really not much choice other than Bally's Park Place.

The Spa at Bally's has a very nice indoor swimming pool and several whirlpools in one central room that is nicely designed with a semi-tropical theme (with plants and few cascading fountains). There are lounge chairs surrounding the pool and private areas for massage therapy. It has fitness and aerobic equipment.

If you need some sporty attire or workout equipment, Bally's **Spa Pro Shop** is located right in the spa area. There is even the **Spa Café** within the confines of the spa area, so you can enjoy a quick and healthy bite while you relax the day away and rejuvenate. And the best part is, the entire facility is open year round.

BALLY'S PARK PLACE - CONCLUSION

Bally's Park Place stands alone in terms of its reasonably-priced accommodations, spa facility, and sheer amount of gambling space. However, when you consider that it is also connected directly to Bally's Wild Wild West Casino to the south and Claridge to the north, this is really a monster of a place. It is one of the most inexpensive resorts in Atlantic City, and definitely the most playful in terms of décor and crowd. It is frequently crowded, and evidently most frequented by the various out-of-town casino junket bus services. Because it's a little more tinselly than the other resorts, don't expect everything to be top-notch quality; it has a worn-down feeling to it that is appealing if you enjoy a more relaxed atmosphere.

THE CLARIDGE

The Claridge hotel, originally built in the 1930s, was renovated for casino use and re-opened in 1981. It is the smallest casino in Atlantic City, a fact that has not been very good for business. In 2002 it was purchased by Bally's and renovated yet again as The Claridge Tower at Bally's. Today, The Claridge Casino Hotel is the only hotel in Atlantic City that has maintained its original look from the city's Heyday (other hotels have either been torn down or extensively re-modeled).

Although it is considered a "Boardwalk Resort", Claridge is not on the boardwalk. Rather, it is one block away, overlooking Brighton Park on the Oceanside, with the view of the Atlantic Ocean further in the distance than most other boardwalk resorts.

ARRIVING AT THE HOTEL

Though now officially a part of Bally's, for a long time Claridge Resort operated independently. So unlike Bally's other arm, the Wild Wild West Casino, Claridge is a complete resort complex with a self-park lot, valet, and accommodations.

Make a left off the Atlantic City Expressway and onto Atlantic Avenue. Proceed just beyond Bally's and follow the signs for the Claridge self-park or valet area. As you probably won't be able to check in directly at Claridge (their front desk is basically useless) you will eventually need to go south to Bally's Park Place and check-in there to receive your room assignment.

Old Hotels and New Hotels

One of the most interesting and eclectic aspects of Atlantic City is the combination of old and new hotels. While many of the resorts on the boardwalk were built since the gambling age, others are radically renovated old hotels from the late 1800s, early-mid 1900s when Atlantic City was the "Queen of Resorts". These old hotels still maintain the exterior's original charm; much the way it probably looked to the vacationers of yore. Of course, the insides are all new.

One of the original requirements for building a resort casino in Atlantic City was that the resort had to be in a newly built facility. The resorts that are in old renovated hotels (such as Claridge and Resorts) were able to by-pass this rule by making significant updates to the interiors, or by adding new wings and expanding.

It is interesting to see the eclectic nature of some of these resorts; since many have been pieced together by upgrades or acquiring and re-modeling older hotels, there is a non-conformity about more than a few of them. Crossing over from a new edition to an old edition may or may not be noticeable, depending on the quality of the patch-and-paint job and the keenness of a discerning eye.

Entering Claridge is much more fun from the boardwalk than from the street. In addition to a nice view of beautiful Brighton Park (with its central water fountain and nearby Korean War Memorial), you will get to ride Atlantic City's longest indoor people-mover – an indoor moving walkway that takes visitors from the boardwalk to the block-away Claridge. Unfortunately, however, the people-mover is only one-way, so getting back over to the boardwalk requires either walking through Brighton Park (not altogether unpleasant) or maneuvering into Bally's and accessing the boardwalk directly from there. Incidentally, this people-mover also connects the boardwalk to Sands Casino Resort, which is also located off the boardwalk.

ACCOMMODATIONS

Claridge rooms are inquired about and booked through the main Bally's Atlantic City office. Sometimes you can choose to stay at Claridge, other times you may be forced to stay at either Bally's Park Place or Claridge, depending on how booked the hotel is for the night. In either case, if you stay at Bally's or Claridge, you have access to all the amenities at either of them.

Claridge rooms are nice and quaint, while still maintaining a decent size. There are various levels of accommodations here as well as at Bally's main resort, but there are significantly less rooms here. Claridge is also one of the best remodeling jobs in all of Atlantic City – the resort maintains an air of the old charm, but still feels fresh and new.

Of particular note at Claridge is the very small but very nice pool and fitness area. It is one of the most intimate and comfortable pool areas, which – if not too crowded – can really be relaxing. There are huge windows that let in an abundance of light (especially if it's sunny) and relaxing lounge chairs with a couple of trees scattered about. Of course, all the standard massage and fitness services are available. The fitness room is very small but it has most of what you'd need to get a good workout.

Though the Spa at Bally's (located at Bally's Park Place) is arguably the crown jewel of pool and spa areas in Atlantic City, the Claridge's intimate environment is a definite plus when you're trying to escape from the bustle of the city. The Spa at Bally's is the most popular but also frequently the busiest.

Unfortunately, however, unlike The Spa at Bally's non-resort-guests cannot use the Claridge facilities. This could also be an advantage; it means less people. Guests of Bally's can use both pools/spas.

Exploring the Resort

For a small resort, Claridge really does pack it in. The tri-level casino area seems unusually difficult to navigate. The stairs and escalators never seem to lead you where you want to go, and if you enter the resort by way of the people-mover, you may find it difficult to find your way back to the mover. Though the people-mover only goes one way, the walkway also connects you to the nearby Sands resort.

The ambience at Claridge however, is small and intimate, with a clean bright look to it, almost like a simple room in a turn-of-the-century single family home, stretched out to casino-size. Everything is closer together, and the walls seem to close in on you after a while. You may feel right at home if you like the smaller yet more confusing layout, but some may find it very claustrophobic, especially if you plan on gambling for a while.

The Caesars Entertainment Comp Program

This book is *not* a guide to gambling, but: Caesars Atlantic City, Bally's Atlantic City (all three sections) and the Atlantic City Hilton all share the same gambling comp program. In fact, all Caesars Entertainment-owned resorts nationwide share the same comp program. If you are gambling for comps and join this "Connection Card" program, the comps you accumulate are good at all eighteen resorts owned by Caesars. It is the most extensive comp program in Atlantic City!

Note: if you gamble a lot at one particular resort, you may be entitled to additional comps at that resort that, unlike the "official" comp program, would not be accepted at the other resorts.

The rooms in the Claridge Tower carry this intimacy to a new level – though they are of decent size, they have a very homey feel to them. They seem to be designed to emulate a guest room in your sweet, loveable grandmother's house. They are totally renovated, so expect them to be new and especially clean-feeling. There are suites available, but the selection is very small. When you book your room at Bally's, you may be able to choose Claridge if there are rooms available.

SHOPPING AND ENTERTAINMENT

Since Bally's Park Place does not have a major performance venue, concerts and other events are held at the Palace Theater at Claridge, which still only accommodates between five and six hundred spectators. The small size makes sense for Claridge since it is a small resort and was once independent.

A smaller entertainment venue in Claridge with free evening and weekend concerts is **Lucky's Bar and Lounge**, located on the third floor. Claridge also has a 24-hour gift shop, called simply **Claridge Gift Shop**, located in the main lobby of the resort (on the ground floor, near the valet entrance). Here, you can purchase various sundries and Claridge-themed gifts.

Claridge also has a swimming pool and spa facility on the eighth floor. It is significantly smaller than The Spa at Bally's next door, but it does feature a small indoor pool, steam room, whirlpool, as well as massage treatments and a fitness center. Claridge's Beauty Salon is also located on the ninth floor. These facilities are rarely as crowded as other resorts' spa areas.

EATING AND DRINKING

Claridge has a steakhouse to call its own as well; **The Twenties Steakhouse**. It has what you'd expect: quality choices of steak and chops, and a nice view. Of special note is the steakhouse's weekly Sunday Brunch – it gets very crowded though, so call in advance for a reservation!

Garden Café takes advantage of the fact that Claridge is not located directly on the boardwalk – it offers a great view of the beautiful Brighton Park and the ocean in the distance. It features a standard menu with all kinds of quick eats, from pizza to stir-fry and sandwiches. The food is not spectacular, but the view of the park is unique.

On your way to Bally's? Coming back to Claridge? Stop at **The Bagel & Doughnut Connection**, which is located on the connecting platform between the two resorts. Kind of like a local New York City bagel shop, you'll find various cheap & filling eats, including ice cream, coffee, and cold beverages (and bagels & doughnuts, of course!).

For another last-minute choice with more substantial eats, Claridge's quick Asian food stop is **The Fulu Noodle Bar**. Located right off the main casino floor, the attraction here is the wide variety of noodle soups. Choices include stew beef, shrimp wonton, spicy chicken leg, and much more. Another choice for fast Asian food is **Wok & Roll**; the chain has a location within Claridge right off the casino floor.

THE CLARIDGE - CONCLUSION

Claridge, being the smallest resort in Atlantic City, has a definite quaint and intimate charm that is simply not available at any other resort in the area. Even the casino floor – an area of gambling resorts that tends to be the most obviously huge, seems small.

However, since Claridge is part of Bally's Atlantic City, you get the best of both worlds: the luxuries of a large resort, but the small, cozy feeling of a small hotel.

SANDS HOTEL & CASINO

Indiana Avenue & Brighton Park
Atlantic City, NJ
(609) 441-4000

Sands Hotel & Casino is a bright, glitzy collage of color – at once both cartoonish and slick. It is a small resort, located immediately north of Claridge, and is the northernmost Casino in Atlantic City's midtown area.

As of 2000, Carl Icahn owns Sands. In the world of hostile corporate takeovers, Icahn is a powerhouse. Known for his takeovers in the 1980s of Texaco, USX, and most notably Trans World Airlines, Icahn currently owns three casinos in Las Vegas – including the iconic Stratosphere, which shares a similar design scheme to Sands.

ARRIVING AT THE HOTEL

Sands Hotel & Casino is located on the boardwalk in the midst of several older buildings, which still have their original, largely unrenovated, exteriors. This provides a unique setting that is visually calmer than the brighter, showier areas of other hotels.

The northernmost resort in the large midtown section of the strip, Sands sits right next to Claridge. And like Claridge, it is not located directly on the boardwalk. But instead of overlooking beautiful Brighton Park, it overlooks an unattractive parking lot. Access to Sands from the boardwalk is via the one-way people mover, which also connects the boardwalk to the Claridge. You can also access Sands directly from the nearby Claridge by way of the same people-mover.

The word that best summarizes the ambience of Sands' interior is neon. The décor is like one giant slot machine - sparkling, flashing lights in a 1950s-ish, neon environment. Everything seems larger than life and colorful neon lights accent almost everything.

The exterior of Sands is not quite up to par with the glimmering interior. There are no good ocean views, the building looks old and the parking lot it overlooks is a major downgrade. In short, don't start forming opinions until you enter and explore a little bit.

ACCOMMODATIONS

Sands has just over six hundred rooms, and consists of two different hotel towers. The first is their classic tower, and the second is the very secluded and newly renovated Madison House hotel, which they call the Madison Tower. Both towers have standard rooms and suites. The Sands also offers nice Jacuzzi suites for romantic getaways.

Access to the Madison Tower is on the same walkway that connects visitors to the self-park garage, behind an almost hidden door, which requires your room key for entry. Although farther away from the main casino and activities, it is definitely quieter and more secluded. The Madison Tower even has its own check-in desk, which is open on a limited basis.

Guests of Sands can enjoy a small and slightly limited health spa, which includes cardiovascular and weight lifting equipment as well as a steam room and sauna.

EATING AND DRINKING

Sands offers a small selection of dining options. The two most upscale restaurants on the property are located on the second floor. **Brighton Steakhouse** has a nice selection of meat and fish. The dining is upscale, but still has a casual atmosphere about it. For Italian Food, there is **Medici**. Both of these locations offer fine dining experiences.

Also on property are two buffet-style eateries, both located on the third floor: **Rossi's Gourmet Italian Buffet** offers choices that are almost exclusively Italian, whereas **Boardwalk Buffet** has standard buffet-style food selections, with a great themed environment reminiscent of the Atlantic City Boardwalk during the turn-of-the-century.

For 24-hour casual dining, **The Corner** has a nice selection of food; more so than other 24-hour eateries in the area. **The Corner Express** is their take-out counter if you wish to eat somewhere else. For fastest and greasiest of foods, **The Grill** (also on the third floor) serves hamburgers, pizza, sandwiches, and other various portable edibles.

Finally, if you don't want an actual meal but need to munch on a snack, **The Peanut Shoppe,** in addition to peanuts, also offers salt water taffy, popcorn, and other snack foods. There is also an on-property **Starbucks**. Both of these snacking options are located near the hotel's lobby.

SHOPPING AND ENTERTAINMENT

Sands has one major venue and two smaller ones. **The Copa Room** is a Las Vegas-style showroom, where you sit at tables while watching the performance. Tickets are required and can be purchased at online ticket vendors or at the box office.

The smaller venues are located within two lounge areas. Music performances are generally free and with scattered show times. **The Copa Lounge**, located right next to The Copa Room, is sleek and dark, with a nice fountain in the entryway and a piano nearby.

And then there's **Swingers.** If you are exploring the casino, even for a little while, you'll almost immediately stumble into this centrally located bar/lounge that stretches up the two floors of the casino with an ultra-high ceiling. The bar is totally open with easy access both to and from the casino; it also has live music on occasion. It is bright and glitzy, like everything else, but not entirely relaxing.

CONCLUSION

The theme of Sands – a mix of classic Atlantic City and neon 1950s design, is one of my favorites. You almost expect to see a drive-in movie theater or a 1950s-style diner. It is probably one of the cheesiest themes in Atlantic City (way up there with Wild Wild West Casino) but done in a much classier, and much aesthetically sharper way. Like Claridge, it is a smaller resort. However, unlike Claridge, the bright neon glitz does not feel so claustrophobic.

There is also not much to see or do on the property other than gamble; but its almost-central location makes for relatively easy access to a plethora of off-property entertainment options. Sands Hotel & Casino itself has a retro, stylish charm all its own, and is well worth a visit.

Resorts Atlantic City

1133 Boardwalk
Atlantic City, NJ
(609) 344-6000

When gambling was finally legalized in Atlantic City in 1976, the first casino to open was Resorts International, a mere 18 months later. Investors had purchased the Chalfonte-Haddon Hall hotel, and instead of building an entirely new resort, only had to do some simple renovations since the old hotel already met the 500-room minimum requirements.

The original hotel had about 1,000 rooms, but the new ownership cut the rooms down to under 600 to make room for the casino floor and other on-site amenities. On May 26th 1978, at 10:00AM, the gambling era in Atlantic City was born, as Resorts International opened its doors.

Over the years, Resorts Atlantic City has had numerous owners, including Donald Trump and Merv Griffin. Today, private investors in Los Angeles own it. It is a complex that holds the unique Atlantic City title as being the first casino.

Arriving at the Hotel

Resorts Atlantic City is the southernmost resort-hotel of the boardwalk's uptown area. As you arrive you'll immediately notice that it has a very classical look. The exterior is almost all white with a little bit of a bluish trim. It looks like an old east coast hotel that has been well preserved, although it is also easy to tell what parts of the complex's exterior are from the original hotel and which parts have been added on.

Because the name of the resort is so generic, the road signs pointing to this area saying "Resorts" might lead to the assumption that the signs are for *all resorts*. Of course, this is not the case, and somebody looking for the Tropicana Resort may unexpectedly wind up at this resort.

Maybe it's because I don't drive very much living in New York City, but I found the self-park garage at Resorts exceptionally difficult to navigate - there were too many sharp turns and inadequate signs. I suggest using valet parking at this one – not because the experience is any better, but because self-park at this location is a real drag.

ACCOMMODATIONS

Resorts Atlantic City has definitely aged despite its "recent" renovation. Though the casino floor sparkles and shines as would be expected, the rest of the hotel clearly echoes the past. Resorts also claim to have the largest standard-sized rooms in Atlantic City. If they are the largest, it is not by a lot.

There are two hotel towers in Resorts. The original hotel that was remodeled into Resorts is the Rendezvous Tower, which has basic accommodations. The visibly newer Ocean Tower has standard size rooms, Jacuzzi suites, and various other levels of rooms and suites.

Resorts also has an indoor-outdoor pool that is open year round in its spa facility. They also have a fitness center, whirlpool, and the other expected spa amenities. They offer massages as well - Swedish, aromatherapy, and more. During summertime these can all be experienced outdoors. Also in the summertime, there is an outdoor bar where you can drink in between pool laps or weight repetitions.

EATING AND DRINKING

Resorts is limited when it comes to the selection of food and drink options. Its close proximity to the much-better-equipped Trump Taj Mahal may prove to be an advantage for those looking for a little more variety in their dining choices.

The best restaurant in Resorts is **Capriccio**. This is an Italian fine dining restaurant, which overlooks the Atlantic Ocean and has a Mediterranean atmosphere. For meatier choices, **Camelot**, with its medieval theme and extensive steak and seafood menu, is a unique and surprising delight, if only for the interesting mix of ambiance and food. Finally, **Asian Spice**, the only other fine dining restaurant in Resorts, offers standard Asian fare (of varying sorts), in a typical setting overlooking the ocean. Asian Spice also features an extensive noodle bar for a quicker, less elegant bite.

There aren't too many casual choices here, either. **The Buffet** is Resorts' main and only significant buffet-style restaurant. It touts an international cuisine, which it delivers, but don't expect too much exotic flare. The **Beach Ball Deli and Seafood House** is exactly what its name suggests – a half deli, half seafood eatery. It is moderately priced and has outside seating during the warmer months. Finally, there is **Breadsticks Café & Grill**, with standard quick-eats such as pizza and sandwiches.

If you're just into having a drink, **Tuxedo's Lobby Bar** is a nice place to sit back for a few quick drinks. On occasion (particularly during the weekend evenings) there is live musical entertainment to enjoy.

SHOPPING AND ENTERTAINMENT

In addition to the occasional live entertainment at Tuxedo's Lobby Bar, Resorts offers two different venues, neither of which are very big. The larger **Superstar Theater** features touring celebrities and musical groups. The smaller **Screening Room** is for more intimate performances. Although the theater can accommodate smaller shows, it is ideally suited for comedy shows (which are frequently featured). Both venues (depending on the acts) require tickets to be purchased in advance.

Resorts has a small selection of shops for those desperate to shop without leaving the hotel. **Caprice** sells collectible knick-knacks of porcelain, costume jewelry, and crystal items. **Talk of the Walk**, a chain of fine women's clothing stores in several Atlantic City resorts, has a store here.

The on-site salon is called **Special Effects**, which has all the standard services of a salon, including hair, nail, and foot care. Finally, for regular sundries and such, **Resorts Gifts and News** sells Atlantic City-themed gifts and whatever last-minute items you may have forgotten.

The newest entertainment complex at Resorts: **Nikki Beach**, an international chain of chill-out places where patrons can drink, bask in a party atmosphere, check out live music, and more.

CONCLUSION

Resorts' place in Atlantic City's casino history definitely makes it worth a visit. But it's an old place. It has changed ownership and identities quite a bit, even by Atlantic City standards, and it seems like a generic place to stay and play. Even the name "Resorts" has an air of disinterest. However, as with the other resorts along the boardwalk, Resorts still has a quality unto itself.

The location on the boardwalk, though not the worst, definitely does not help. Since it is the southernmost resort in the uptown area (just south of Taj Mahal), it requires some walking to get down to the central resort area. Since there's not a lot to do, eat, or drink in Resorts you may find yourself wanting to wander off a little more frequently.

Trump Taj Mahal

1000 Boardwalk at Virginia Avenue
Atlantic City, NJ
(609) 449-1000

The third and newest of the three Donald Trump resorts in Atlantic City, Trump Taj Mahal is the most noticeable and largest in the uptown area. Until the Borgata was completed in 2003, the Trump Taj Mahal was also the newest resort in Atlantic City – a title it held for about thirteen years.

Due to the position and size of the building, it is also the most recognizable resort on the boardwalk, and can be seen from miles away. As the somewhat egocentric name suggests, the Trump Taj Mahal is heavily themed with Indian royalty – and the most intricately themed of all the Trump Resorts. It encompasses over seventeen acres of almost entirely enclosed space, and it is one of the tallest buildings in New Jersey. This, coupled with one of the largest casino floors in the country, makes Trump Taj Mahal indeed a monster of a resort.

Arriving at the Hotel

Follow the signs to the Uptown section of Atlantic City, and you'll immediately notice the Taj Mahal towering over the surrounding resorts. It's the second-northernmost resort on the boardwalk, so expect to be a little bit out of the way from the central pier area.

While valet parking is available, using it will not improve your perception of this resort, so you might as well self-park (or take a bus, if you prefer). Either way, you're pretty much dumped right into the casino, so you'll have to maneuver around a little bit to find the hotel's main lobby.

If you've been to other Trump resorts in the area before, one of your first impressions of the Taj will be that it's the least tinselly-looking of any of his casinos. Though it still glitters of tacky gold wealth, the incredibly bright color palette of the building's interior and exterior subdues that Trump-style. It definitely feels Trump, but a little bit differently.

ACCOMMODATIONS

As the tallest building in Atlantic City, one would expect the Trump Taj to boast the largest number of rooms. On the contrary, the resort has about 1,200 rooms and suites – about as many as Caesars. In addition the standard rooms, the Taj offers a variety of themed suites from which to decide.

Of course, a majority of the rooms are regular guest quarters. But if you want more square footage for your relaxation, you could splurge on an 850 square-foot Viceroy Suite, all the way up to one of their six 2,100 square-foot hospitality suites. Of course, expect to pay through the nose for luxuries like those.

Additionally, guests at the Trump Taj have an indoor pool and a fitness/spa facility to enjoy during their stay.

EATING AND DRINKING

There are about twelve restaurants and lounges in Trump Taj Mahal, ranging from casual meals and drinks to top-of-the-line quality food and service.

If you're in the mood for some fine Asian cuisine, then the best place in Trump Taj is **Dynasty**. Here they have all sorts of oriental food choices, including a nice selection of sushi and maki. Expect to pay a lot, though – this is not casual dining. Dynasty also includes **Moon**, a place to drink and meet in a secluded place during the late night, with other sushi lovers.

If you want to spend lots of money on food, you can also visit the Italian-themed **Mark Anthony's**. Here, they serve all kinds of Italian dishes, with an emphasis on brick oven pizza and tradition pasta entrees.

Lastly in the gourmet category is **Scheherazade**. This is sort of a generic high-quality restaurant with an eclectic mix of entrees (they have great lobster!). What really makes it special is the fact that you can eat while overlooking Trump Taj's Baccarat pit! The Trump website claims that this restaurant is the only one in the world where you can watch baccarat while you dine.

Trump Taj Mahal is also home to Atlantic City's **Hard Rock Café**! In the same vein as the Planet Hollywood at Caesars, here you can dine among famous pieces of rock memorabilia. The menu is the same as other Hard Rocks, and the prices are just as inflated. But it is a lot of fun. Hard Rock Café is located directly on the boardwalk, so if it's warm you can choose their outdoor eating area.

There are several other chain restaurants in Trump Taj Mahal as well. The **Stage Deli of New York** has locations both in Atlantic City and midtown Manhattan and **Sbarro** has locations all over the United States.

Since every resort-casino has to have some kind of a buffet, the Trump Taj has the **Sultan's Feast**. This newly renovated restaurant has what you would expect from an Atlantic City buffet, including the inflated prices. Finally, if you're just looking for an easy-going coffeehouse-style facility, the **Bombay Café** will grill (or steam, or wrap up) what you desire to eat, twenty-four hours a day.

Finally, if you're just looking for a drink, or a place to relax, then **The Oasis** is perfect for you. This lounge also features live entertainment from time to time.

SHOPPING AND ENTERTAINMENT

There are lots of things to do at Trump Taj Mahal – more so than many of the other resorts. Unlike the Atlantic City Hilton located on the far opposite end of the strip, Trump Taj compensates for its more remote location with a host of great attractions and diversions! Though Trump Taj is not quite as remote as the Hilton, it definitely picks up where the Hilton left off.

For a family-friendly destination, Trump Taj Mahal is a great choice – better than most other resorts in the area. In addition to the incredibly close proximity to the **Steel Pier** amusement area (see the Steel Pier section elsewhere in this book), it also has one of only a few on-resort video arcades, called **Ali Baba's Arcade**. Though the arcade is very small and not as packed with games as the casino not ten feet away, it is definitely a step in the right direction for a multi-functional resort.

Want to do some Taj shopping? There are some great choices for finer (and overpriced, as usual) apparel and fashionable merchandise. **Barron Leather** specializes in designed handbags and leather apparel. For the men, the **B. Gentlemen** has some great upscale choices. **Caché** has a store here as well, for women's attire, and **Bernie Robbins** has a nice collection of expensive jewelry and watches. Head for **Bath Junkie** for interesting herbal and aromatic bath and body products. Finally, for the motorcycle lover, shop at the **Harley-Davidson Store** for branded merchandise.

Are you hungry for a very quick bite? On the Taj property you'll find an **Auntie Anne's** pretzel shop, **Boardwalk Treats** for on-the-go hot dogs, ice cream, and more, and **Beka's Pastry Shop** for coffee products and various baked goods.

But no trip to a resort would be complete without some branded merchandise to prove you were there. **Exclusively Taj** has printed their logo on all sorts of great but mostly pointless gift ideas.

Trump Taj Mahal has two large venues to host a variety of events. **The Arena** seats a whopping 5,000 guests, and the smaller **Xanadu** Showroom can hold up to 1,400. Check with the resort's box office for more information on events and shows.

Last, but definitely not least, there's **Casbah** – Trump Taj's answer to New York City's Webster Hall. In this mega dance club that is hyped on billboards all across Trump Taj and the rest of Atlantic City, you can dance the night away with a huge assortment of young travelers, many of which seem to have never been to a dance club before. If you like large and sweaty dance floors with flashing lights and pretty dancers, then Casbah is a great place to be. The drinks are expensive, and the **Casbah Café** nearby serves all kind of munchies, but it really is a large and enjoyable club. This is a strictly tourist club, however – there are other places where locals go.

Conclusion

Trump Taj Mahal is a grand resort, with many things to see and do beyond gambling. It's a comfortable and happy place with a very unique design and consistency throughout. Too bad it is located so far north on the strip.

If you don't have a car and do not intend to leave your resort, then this is an ideal place. There is so much to do within Taj that you won't really need to leave. This is not true for most of the other resorts, where you may end up needing to explore a bit for the sheer lack of things to do within the confines.

SHOWBOAT ATLANTIC CITY

801 Boardwalk
Atlantic City, NJ
(609) 343-4000

Showboat is billed as "The Mardi Gras Casino", but it really has a more general New Orleans theme. It is owned and operated by Bill Harrah's casino namesake chain, now the largest Casino resort chain in the world (including its recent acquisition of Caesars Entertainment). Harrah's operates a total of two casinos in Atlantic City.

The Showboat originally opened in 1987. Since Resorts International owns much of the property uptown, the land on which Showboat is built has been leased from them. Harrah's, much later (in 1998), purchased the casino chain.

Showboat was once one of Atlantic City's smallest resorts, but a recent renovation added an entirely new hotel tower and over five hundred additional rooms, bringing the total to well over a thousand. The casino floor is long and thin (as is the resort itself), and most major activities are located on the sides of the main level.

ARRIVING AT THE HOTEL

Showboat is the northernmost resort on the Atlantic City boardwalk. After exiting the Atlantic City Expressway, make a left and drive down Atlantic Avenue until the very end of the resort complex. If you'll notice, right beyond Showboat, there is a very large, very ugly empty lot. While this seems to be an unfortunate location for Showboat (and for the time being it is) there are some big plans in the works for this lot – plans that have been in effect for a while, so for the time being, vacationers will simply have to put up with it.

The driving entrance to Showboat does a good job of blocking out the surrounding environment. The valet parking requires that you enter a circular driveway that is blocked on all sides by the Showboat building. If you're using valet, pull into the circular driveway and around to the underpass.

When you enter the main doors, you're immediately presented with the front desk, and – ta-da! – New Orleans! There is a small bandstand in the center of the check-in area to entertain while you wait, and the color scheme and trim are of the true New Orleans Style, particular of the French Quarter. While there is nothing inherently "Mardi Gras" about the area, it definitely oozes "good time."

ACCOMMODATIONS

The Showboat is a pleasant surprise. Though small and awkwardly located, the entire facility is very well taken care of. Showboat has two towers; one opened with the original hotel and the other is the result of a multi-million dollar renovation, which was completed in mid-2003. Showboat offers several different levels of room styles and well over two hundred suites. The cream of the crop for their room selection is the two Super Suites, which are basically entire houses – very large.

Resort guests also have access to the **Big Easy Spa** and pool facilities. The spa features basic workout equipment and tanning booths, steam baths, Jacuzzis, saunas, and other amenities (including massages, by appointment). The pool is outdoors and thus is seasonal. The outdoor deck is small, with little more than a few deck chairs. Salon International is also available for your various beautification requirements (hair, nails, and skin care).

EXPLORING THE RESORT

After walking through the street entrance and passing the hotel check-in area, you'll notice that there is no place you can go other than straight.

Showboat (including the casino floor) is long and thin, which makes it one of the easiest resorts to navigate. As the hotel stretches back, one long side is reserved strictly for casino activity, while the other side has some of the various restaurants and activities.

The New Orleans theme is carried nicely throughout the stretch – there are various street scenes, facades, and other visual treats that shout "party". As you walk near the back – towards the boardwalk – you'll encounter New Orleans Square. This is a small section of the property that features a ground-level bar nearby and a small bandstand, which frequents live performances. This is an exquisite section, which mimics (on a smaller scale) the style of Bally's Wild Wild West Casino.

The New Orleans-style façade in this section is multi-level; with the walls decorated to look like the exteriors of French Quarter buildings, and well-dress mannequins appearing to wave at the crowd below. This is a great little section of the resort; comparable in quality to the lobby area of Caesars Atlantic City. Overall, Showboat maintains the New Orleans ("Mardi Gras") atmosphere throughout, from the well-decorated but small lobby in the front to the very well appointed New Orleans Square in the back.

EATING AND DRINKING

Since Showboat is one of the smaller resorts, choices for dining and beverage service are somewhat restricted. In fact, if you want a more upscale dinner, you're really better off heading nearby to the Trump Taj Mahal, as the only upscale restaurant in Showboat is **Rib & Chophouse**; which isn't all that upscale (it is billed as "casual/dressy", which could mean anything but shorts & tee shirt). It features what one expects; many choices of meat served many different ways.

The best place to dine by far at Showboat is the **French Quarter Buffet**. It is definitely one of the best buffets in Atlantic City, and the only one where most of the food is actually prepared right in front of you. The ambiance is that of a New Orleans street (think Bourbon Street but without the indiscretions); it has recently been remodeled to include more seats.

Other more casual on-site options include **Casa Di Napoli**, which features Italian food, and **Noodle Bar (actually on the casino floor)**, which has casual Asian food. **Canal Street Bread and Sandwich**

Co. serves easy snack-type foods, such as sandwiches and pizza. If you're hungry at 2:00AM, have no fear: **Mansion Café** serves food 24-hours a day. If you only want a drink, the only real choice (other than free drinks for gamblers on the casino floor) is **The Beach Bar** – a kind of California sports bar, which... fits in with Mardi Gras?

And there's also a **Starbucks**. You know what to expect.

Shopping and Entertainment

Except for the casino and the very nice French Quarter decorations, there is little to do in Showboat. On occasion they host live shows or events, but there is rarely, if ever, any headlining entertainment. Tickets for the events in their showroom can be purchased using online ticket vendors.

There are a mere two shops worthy of mention in Showboat. The **Ocean 11 Gift Shop** is their gift and sundries station with branded merchandise and a generally utilitarian product line. The other shop – **Boardwalk Peanut Shoppe** – features lots of great sweets, especially salt-water taffy and peanuts.

Conclusion

Showboat Atlantic City has an unfortunate location, especially given that it is one of the better resorts in the area. There is literally nothing north of Showboat on the boardwalk; not a single store, not a single hotel. The Garden Pier is nearby, as well as the Absecon Lighthouse (if you're willing to walk a bit or have access to a car). Otherwise, you'll have to either go south or leave Atlantic City for nearby Brigantine.

It is also a very surprising resort. The exterior gives little indication as to the theme and style of the interior. Parts of it really are accurate New Orleans, much more so than Bally's Wild Wild West is cowboyville, and more comparable to reality than Caesars.

THE MARINA DISTRICT RESORTS

Although the Atlantic City boardwalk is by far the most famous and well-traveled section of the city, there is another area that definitely deserves attention – the Marina District. Specifically, the Marina District is a set of three resort-hotels that do not reside on the boardwalk.

The Marina Disadvantage / Advantage

The Marina District of Atlantic City has two major strikes against it: the resort-hotels are not located on the boardwalk (and thus not accessible by foot from the other casinos), and they cannot be accessed any way other than by car, taxicab or Atlantic City Jitney (no New York City bus). While this may seem like a disadvantage, it has actually forced these resorts to achieve a level of quality that makes people want to leave the boardwalk and pay them a visit. In other words, with few exceptions, these are three of the best resorts in Atlantic City.

The resorts in the Marina District are: Trump Marina, Harrah's Atlantic City, and the Borgata. This section will describe this section of the city, and the reasons why you should definitely check out these three extraordinary resorts.

Getting to the Marina District is easy from the other casinos. Simply follow the signs on Atlantic or Pacific Avenue to the "Marina". You will eventually make your way onto the Atlantic City Connector, which takes you underground and basically dumps you at any one of the three marina casinos before crossing over to Brigantine. Traffic permitting, you can get from anywhere on the boardwalk to the marina district in less than five minutes.

So jump in your car and let's drive over to the Marina District!

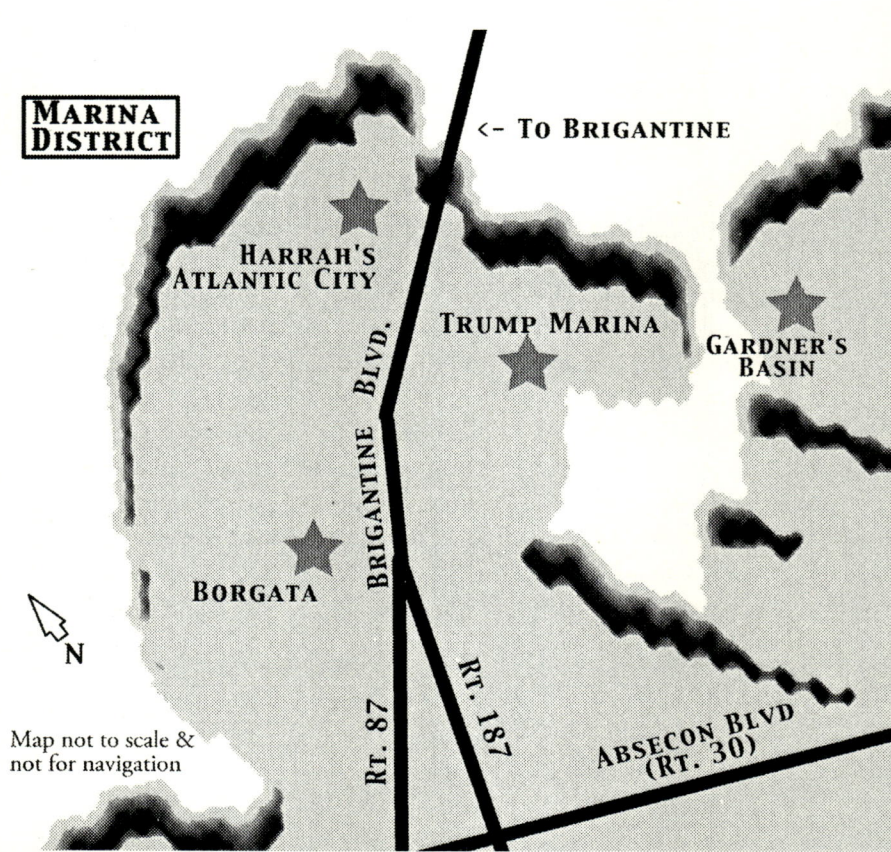

Map not to scale & not for navigation

Harrah's Atlantic City

777 Harrah's Blvd
Atlantic City, NJ
(609) 441-5600

After the 2004 acquisition of Caesars Entertainment, the Harrah's corporation is now the largest gaming resort entity in the world. However, even before that, it had operated many resorts all over the country. Unlike other casino chains, which may require visitors to travel great distances to experience, many parts of the country actually have a Harrah's nearby. Sometimes it is a casino-hotel, sometimes it is just a casino, and sometimes it is a boat. In any case, Harrah's has sort of grown up to be a very accessible casino chain, with one of the friendliest, least intimidating atmospheres. Harrah's Atlantic City is one of the two resorts in the area managed directly by Harrah's - the other being Showboat, discussed prior.

Arriving and Checking In

Follow the signs to the Marina District. Although all three resorts in this area are close-by, you cannot walk to them. The exit for Harrah's is the last one on Brigantine Boulevard before driving over the water into Brigantine. Although Harrah's Atlantic City is the only establishment located on Harrah's Boulevard, they have decided to address it 777. Feeling lucky yet?

The main entrance and valet parking area kind of, sort of resembles a mansion on an old southern estate. Since Harrah's has always attempted to be a very accessible and friendly casino, dressing up to resemble the friendly South fits well its intent.

The check-in desk is located way on the other side of the main entryway, which – if you look up – has an interesting dome shape and a stained-glass ornamental structure vaguely reminiscent of Mohegan Sun's casino architecture in Connecticut. As you walk to the front desk, on the left you'll see a good portion of the casino itself.

ACCOMMODATIONS

Harrah's Atlantic City has over sixteen hundred rooms and suites in four different small "towers" – Bayview, Atrium, Marina, and Harbour. While they all have various room types, the Bayview tower is the most upscale. Depending on availability, you may be able to choose your tower.

Despite the potential for a large resort feel, Harrah's is actually much smaller and plainer than the other Marina District resorts. It has a very relaxed atmosphere; it is lightly decorated and there are comfortable couches and other places to sit scattered about the facility. For a larger resort, it really feels small and manageable. Most amenities are located right off the casino floor, on the main lobby level.

SHOPPING AND ACTIVITIES

There are only a few places to do any kind of serious shopping at Harrah's. Of course there's the standard **Harrah's Gift Shop**, with sundries and products, many stamped with Harrah's insignia. Also, **Talk of the Walk**, a chain of fine women's apparel in Atlantic City, has a location here. Also, **The David Charles Salon** is on property for your beautification needs. The Salon caters to both men and women with hairstyling, manicures, pedicures, and facials.

Harrah's Atlantic City also has a small indoor pool, which is open year-round. The pool is part of a **Fitness Center**, which has aerobic, and fitness equipment, a sauna, and a Jacuzzi. During the summer, there is also an outdoor sun deck. The center has ping-pong, shuffleboard, and even mini golf.

Harrah's is also home to one of only a few in-resort arcade game centers for children and teenagers. **The Teen Center**, right above the casino, has a few arcade games and activities to keep young ones active while the grown-ups gamble. Unlike the casino, however, The Teen Center is not open 24 hours a day.

EATING AND DRINKING

Harrah's Atlantic City has several fine dining experiences on its property. **'CESCA** is their Italian restaurant. The food here is a wide selection of contemporary Italian dishes (including meat and pasta). **The Steakhouse** is more exclusively carnivorous, with steaks, chops and others prepared in a variety of ways. Harrah's recommends that reservations be made in advance for their two fine dining eateries. Next to The Steakhouse is **Bluepoint**, a raw bar with a shellfish selection, as well as some seafood and drinks.

For the more casual diner, the **Reflections Café** and **Corner Grille** serve more standard fare, such as hamburgers and pizza. Reflections is open 24 hours a day. Harrah's buffet is the **Fantasea Reef Buffet**, which has a great underwater decor. Enjoy not just seafood, but a wide variety of choices for breakfast, lunch, and dinner. The most unique aspect of this buffet is, of course, the well-conceived well-executed sea theme.

For drinks and a little more, **Club Cappuccino** features a wide array of coffees and some light eating choices (such as sandwiches and sweets). For drinks and perhaps some entertainment check out the newer **EDEN LOUNGE** and **Xibition Bar** (located on the casino floor).

CONCLUSION

Harrah's Atlantic City is the smallest resort in the Marina District, which means that to expand your options of entertainment, you would require a trip in your car, a cab, or a Jitney. On-property, you are limited to a few select shops and attractions, but probably not enough to keep you confined to this resort for the duration of your trip.

On the other hand, a major plus to Harrah's is its massive chain of sister resorts across the country. There are Harrah's in Kansas City,

East Chicago, Lake Tahoe, New Orleans, St. Louis, and many other places, not to mention Las Vegas. Harrah's also owns the chains of Rio, Showboat (in Atlantic City) and Harveys. It is one of the most well-known brands of casino resort in the country. If you feel at home at any other Harrah's, you will definitely feel right at home here as well.

    It is also an ideal location, in its proximity to beautiful Brigantine, just over the bridge. If your plans call for some quality Jersey Shore exploration, Brigantine is definitely one of the better places – it is quiet and peaceful and just around the corner.

Borgata Hotel Casino & Spa

1 Borgata Way
Atlantic City, NJ
(609) 317-1000

The newest casino in 13 years (opened to the public in the summer of 2003), the Borgata is a joint venture between private investors and the MGM Mirage Corporation, which also owns hotels in Las Vegas (the MGM Grand, The Mirage, and Bellagio). Incidentally, as of this writing, MGM Mirage is in the planning stages of another Atlantic City resort adjacent to the Borgata.

Since the Borgata is not located on the boardwalk strip, a car or a taxicab (or Jitney) is a must. Casino buses from New York City do not go to the Marina District at all. Because of this, the Borgata must shine in many ways to convince the wayward traveler to spend the extra time and money to visit this resort as opposed to the other, more easily accessible ones.

In this respect, it has definitely done its job. In fact, the Borgata is the best overall resort in all of Atlantic City – it is the cleanest, nicest, and friendliest (and most expensive). As you'll see, it has a design of a complete destination; not just a gambling resort – even the name has the word "Spa" in it – so they are trying to cater to many different types of vacationers.

Arriving at the Hotel

When driving east on the Atlantic City Expressway, just before entering the city limits, look to the distant left and you will see a tall, thin structure. It has a metallic surface and appears smooth; almost like a large factory pipe among many smaller buildings. This is the Borgata; but don't start forming your opinions just yet.

As you continue driving, you'll notice that the Borgata is actually a wide but basically flat building. The metallic structure shines of brassy gold, and the large "Borgata" sign glued to the top of the hotel comes into view. Follow the signs leading to the Marina District of Atlantic City.

Although you can utilize the self-park garage, again it is advantageous (for the sake of first impressions) to use the valet parking entrance. Pull right up to the main driveway of the resort, and hand an attendant your keys. Then proceed through the main doors.

When you first enter the hotel, you're immediately presented with the casino floor – but before you proceed left to the check-in desk, take a look around. Though without much theme (as in ancient Rome or the Wild Wild West), it is a *beautiful* hotel. The floor and decorations are sharp and sparkling. The color scheme is calm and pleasing (light and gentle colors). The decorations – though contemporary – are pleasing and blend in well with the unique environment. It definitely feels like the Bellagio – you might as well be in Las Vegas.

The entire resort has a scheme which is designed to be soothing and comforting – the advertisements on billboard approaching the Borgata point to this. This is unique from other resorts in the area, which are intended to be active hubbubs to play and drink.

Accommodations

Immediately to the left of the entrance is the front desk. After you check in and receive your room key, walk around the perimeter of the casino until you reach the elevators up to your room. For now, although the hotel's main fun areas are only steps away, you will bypass the excitement as you move into your room.

Atlantic City: Beyond Gambling   119

> ### The Borgata at Night
>
> The Borgata is a unique-looking building at any time of day, but if you arrive when it's dark outside, you get a special treat. The entire building glows a calm, dark purple. Though gold and metallic during the day, the building is set up to glow at night in such a unique way that it can be viewed and recognized for many miles. It is really a calming and pleasant design.
>
> Definitely quality tack.

You must show the guard your room key to gain admission to this elevator area, called The Living Room. Around the elevators there are big comfy couches, and a tobacco bar where guests are allowed to smoke and drink and read and enjoy themselves. This area is only for hotel guests, so it is rarely as crowded as the casino itself.

When you're done relaxing, hop into the next elevator and head up to your room. The Borgata's rooms are the best in Atlantic City and among the better rooms of hotels in general. They are large, clean, the pillows and comforters are soft and comfortable. When you first open the door to your room you will immediately notice that everything seems, well, a bit more comfortable than most other hotel rooms.

In many of the standard rooms, there are no bathtubs, but instead there is a walk-in shower (complete with bench) where – if you were so inclined, multiple people could shower comfortably and simultaneously. The water drips daintily from overhead, like a gentle rainfall. Indeed, the whole room is based on your comfort. And it is very successful.

Like other resort-hotels in Atlantic City, the Borgata offers several different levels of suites – though they usually cater to high-rollers. They even have residences available where you can host lavish dinner parties – and a dining room to seat twelve people. Granted, these rooms are ultra-expensive (and ultra-excessive at up to five thousand square feet), in a hotel that is already among the area's most expensive.

Exploring the Grounds

Most of the entertainment at the Borgata is located, or accessible via, the main floor of the resort – the same area where you first checked in. It is basically one large circular room, with a walkway that circumvents the main casino floor in the middle. It is from this area that you can access the various clubs, restaurants, and venues that make up the Borgata's wide array of entertainment possibilities.

Let's begin by heading down the elevator from your room, and entering the main floor by way of **The Living Room**. Around the circumference of the casino floor is a path that connects you to almost every entertainment or eating/drinking opportunity of the resort. I call this "The Ring" but it really doesn't have a name.

As you make a left out of the Living Room, make another immediate left and you have entered the **Retail Piazza**. Here is where the majority of the Borgata's retail shops are located. It is a very pretty area, sort of reminiscent of the same company's much larger shops at Bellagio in Las Vegas. There aren't many stores hare, and the prices are beyond expensive; but it's a lot of fun to look around for a while at this classy mall-esque corner of the resort.

Further down The Ring are several high-quality restaurants and bars. The first ones you pass are **Speccio** (main level) and **Ombra** (downstairs). Both feature quality Italian food, but Ombra is primarily concerned with fine wine. The restaurant itself is designed to look like a huge wine cellar, with thousands of bottles of wine protected behind glass not ten feet from where you dine. The portions are small and expensive; but the wine list is very large. If steak is more your thing, go right next door to the **Old Homestead**, where there is little else on the menu.

These restaurants are fine dining experiences. If you just want a drink or a more casual food option, then the **Gypsy Bar** or the **Borgata Buffet** should be perfect. Gypsy Bar primarily serves beverages, but there is also a small assortment of food if you have the munchies for something other than buffet-style mashed potatoes and corn.

If you just want to drink, check out **B-Bar** and **Mixx**, located clear on the other side of the Ring. Both these places seem to be especially busy in the evening. Mixx actually becomes somewhat of a nightclub in the later hours.

There are several other choices of dining or drinking along The Ring; **The Metropolitan** is open 24 hours a day and has a heavy French-type cuisine influence. Step off The Ring and into the casino and you will hit **N.O.W.** – cheaper Asian eats (noodles and such). **Risi Bisi** offers a relatively inexpensive Italian alternative to the formal Speccio and Ombra. Finally, the **Amphora Lounge** is a good place to eat; but you can stick around after the food is gone, since it is very much a relaxing lounge as well.

ENTERTAINMENT

The Borgata has two major venues on its property. The smaller one is **The Music Box**, which seats about nine hundred people. Though the name suggests a musical experience, The Music Box actually hosts several different kinds of events on an ongoing basis. Of particular note is the Borgata Comedy Club, which uses The Music Box to feature local comedians (and – on occasion – a few headliners).

The larger venue in the Borgata is **The Event Center** – a very large theater which can seat over three thousand people. The Event Center handles all kinds of performances, from music to comedy and everything in between – whatever is touring at the time.

Both of these facilities are accessible right off the Borgata ring on the main floor. The Borgata Box Office has information about what shows are coming and what the ticket prices are. The Borgata Comedy Club is the only recurring show as of this writing; there is a rotation of comics.

MIXX BY DAY AND NIGHT

Mixx is located in the far corner of the Borgata's main casino floor. It consists of two floors, two different bar areas, and several separate, private rooms. As the name suggests; it is a "mix" of personalities, both in purpose and practice.

By day, it's a multi-national restaurant and bar, with a very wide selection of food and drink (particularly wine, though rum and sake are also prevalent) choices. The food is a combination of Asian and Latin cuisine.

By night, Mixx becomes one mega dance club; perhaps the biggest in all of Atlantic City. Like Casbah in Taj Mahal, the Mixx nightclub has the ambiance of Webster Hall in New York City, or even Pleasure Island at Walt Disney World. It is definitely a cheesy club, but definitely, definitely a happening place. It' one of the biggest non-gambling destinations at the Borgata. So if you're young (or young at heart) and want to break your eardrums in one of the largest social gatherings in Atlantic City, and it's a busy weekend, you'll definitely want to check out Mixx, either by day or by night.

BORGATA'S SPA

Sure, it's a casino too, but the Borgata is also a high-quality spa (and fitness center, and general relaxation station, called **Spa and Gardens**). Though most of the resorts in Atlantic City claim to have some kind of spa or pool facility, they sometimes do not live up to the expectations of spas in other, non-casino hotels in other resort areas (except for Las Vegas). Borgata's Spa really lives up to its claims.

The spa is several different facilities that are all located on the second floor of the resort-hotel. The largest and most obvious section (when you first get off the elevators) is the large indoor pool and outdoor sun tanning/relaxing patio (which the Borgata calls the "Gardens"). The pool area is usually not very crowded, but if it is, expect a lot of children whose parents are gambling elsewhere.

The Borgata also has the classic spa services - massages, aromatherapy, you name it – at its **Spa Toccare**. Or, if you want a haircut, visit the **Pierra & Carlo Salon**, or the **Shaving Grace** barbershop.

CONCLUSION

The Borgata is arguably the best – and most expensive – resort in Atlantic City. It especially caters to non-gamblers, because of the abundance of high quality restaurants and the spa area. The spa is one of the two best in Atlantic City – the Spa at Bally's comes very close in terms of facilities and style, but the Borgata has a slight edge, probably because it is has that newer shine about it.

A major downside to the Borgata is the fact that it's not located on the boardwalk – you cannot walk to it, since you'd have to cross several major expressways – and no bus goes there. However, this may turn out to be a blessing since it forces the Borgata to be more of an all-encompassing resort, in order to keep people satisfied about staying off the boardwalk.

What is in the future for Borgata? As mentioned earlier, MGM Mirage seems to be in some planning stages for a major presence in Atlantic City. Borgata may be expanding (the road encircling the large empty lot next to Borgata is called MGM Mirage Boulevard), and the large, empty property north of Showboat is long overdue. As with the rest of Atlantic City, change is brewing, and it is exciting.

TRUMP MARINA

Huron & Brigantine Blvd.
Atlantic City, NJ
(609) 441-2000

Trump Marina was the second of Trump's three Atlantic City Casinos to open. It was initially called Trump Castle, but the name was changed after pressure from then Park Place Entertainment to prevent confusion between it and Caesars Palace in Las Vegas.

Trump Marina, located directly on the water of Absecon Channel, is also home to the Senator Frank S. Farley State Marina, with over six hundred slips available to park a boat or yacht. Though Trump does not own outright the Farley State Marina, it is under their management and integrated directly with the resort. This is the only major resort in Atlantic City with a legitimate marina.

ARRIVING AND ACCOMMODATIONS

Trump Marina is located in the Marina District; so take the Atlantic City Connector for fastest access. It is the closet Marina District Resort to the water, though there is no actual beach access. Instead, as you pull up to the main entrance, you will pass on your left the resort itself, and on the right the Farley State Marina. Enter the Marina underpass.

Walking into the main entrance brings you almost directly into the heart of the resort. The central atrium encompasses three floors, which are connected via a central escalator. The inherent Trump-ness is all there: the chandeliers, the gold-paneled everything, the shiny decorations. Above the central atrium is a large skylight that brings brightness into the resort that makes it feel very friendly and accommodating.

The front desk is located near the back of the main casino floor; it is not in a room of its own and is in a somewhat un-pronounced section. Walking left from the front desk will take you to some of the shopping experiences in Trump Marina, as well as the Grand Cayman ballroom.

The resort has two towers and contains a total of about eight hundred rooms, making it the smallest resort in the Marina District of Atlantic City. The Bay Tower is the largest tower, and where most of the standard accommodations are, including a few suites. However, the Crystal Tower is exceptionally decadent, the most choices of rooms and suites.

If you are staying at Trump Marina during the summer, you may have access to their outdoor pool, which is open seasonally and weather-permitting.

EATING AND DRINKING

For top-of-the-line Trump dining, there is none better than **Portofino**. With great views of both the harbor and the Atlantic City skyline, Portofino offers Italian food. **Harbor View**, located directly next to the Farley Marina, also provides stunning views and specializes in a variety of seafood.

If a view of the marina or harbor is not a priority, you could try the fine **Imperial Court**, which specializes in Asian cuisine of varying sorts. Traveling from East to West, **High Steaks** is the Trump Marina steakhouse; with a variety of quality meat cuts in a traditional western setting.

Casual dining choices are also available at Trump Marina. For one there's the resort's token buffet-style restaurant. The **Bayside Buffet** features standard buffet food on a rotating basis. For pizza and quick eats, **Cosimo's Pizza Café** serves up a variety. The **Upstairs Café**, open 24 hours a day, serves up sandwiches and other last-minute bites.

Trump Marina is also home to one of Atlantic City's two **Hooters** restaurants – the other one being in Tropicana (you can never be too far from a Hooters in Atlantic City). Finally, **The Deck** is an outdoor bar and restaurant. Open seasonally, it is the answer to the boardwalk resorts' on-beach bars, and features occasional live music.

SHOPPING AND ENTERTAINMENT

Trump Marina has four entertainment venues. The largest, **Grand Cayman**, is a ballroom that can be converted for use by many different types of entertainment events (on a personal note: I saw "Weird Al" Yankovic perform there). The second main venue is **The Shell**, which is smaller but has a more traditional showroom layout. Both of these venues tend to hold headliner performances, and both will probably require tickets to be purchased in advanced to attend the events contained therein.

The Wave is a flashy Trump nightclub – but don't expect Trump Taj Mahal's Casbah. The Wave is smaller and more intimate, with an adequate sound system. The Wave is set up to accommodate both live musicians and a D.J. Finally, **The Deck** (open seasonally) offers free live performances in an outdoor environment.

Trump Marina has a small but nice selection of shops and food & drink stands. The Atlantic City women's clothing and accessories chain **Talk of the Walk** has a location here, as well as **Bernie Robbins Fine Jewelry**, with watches, jewelry, and such.

The **Mariner's Gift Shop** is Trump Marina's signature gift shop, with logo-stamped items, food, and sundries. For beauty, the on-property beauty salon is **Dino Roberts**, will all the standard beautification treatments for hair, face, nails, and whatever else that may need beautifying (reservations recommended but not required).

For quick bites, the **Boardwalk Peanut Shoppe** serves all sorts of candies, chocolates, and other delectable goodies. **Auntie Anne's** sells some of the best soft pretzels money can buy, in many flavors.

THE SENATOR FRANK S. FARLEY STATE MARINA

The most unique aspect of Trump Marina is the fact that it really does contain a marina – something rarely associated with traditional casino resort-hotels. The Senator Frank S. Farley State Marina is fully functional. It has electric and water services for yachts and cabin cruisers, gasoline pumps, showers, laundry, and bathroom facilities. The marina itself is owned by the New Jersey Division of Parks and Forestry, so it is not an "official" part of Trump Marina's property.

If you like the Jersey Shore and own a boat, there is really not a better location than the Farley State Marina. It is located in a well-protected inlet with very little waves or water turbulence, the water itself is deep, and many of the Jersey Shore attractions are accessible, as the marina itself is somewhat centrally-located on the shore.

The marina building is clearly separated from the rest of the resort – a walkway takes pedestrians over the main auto entrance road to the marina. There are over six hundred slips for your water vessel to park. These slips can be rented in a variety of ways (for the day or for the summer, and for everything in between). **Docksider** is the Marina's official store, which sells all sorts of useful nautical thingamajigs.

The Farley State Marina is indeed a unique attachment to a casino resort, and worth looking at, even if you don't own a boat.

CONCLUSION

Trump Marina has a glow about it that makes the ambience a little friendlier than the rest of the Trump Resort. The skylight in the main atrium, though not unsurpassed, is a definite plus. (The name "Marina" suggests the nautical outdoors, and the skylight brings some of that outdoors inside).

It is unique that a legitimate marina is attached to this resort, as it provides that additional nautical "flair". Though the resort does not explore the possibility of a true nautical-themed casino resort (there is nothing nautical about this resort except for the marina, which is separated by a walkway), it is definitely one of the brighter and friendlier resorts in Atlantic City. Unfortunately, it is small with no swim-able beach access and not much to do on-property besides gambling.

Off-Resort

Amusement Centers

Roller Coasters. Midway arcades. Redemption Games. Hot dogs and cotton candy. Atlantic City's boardwalk has a history of being jam-packed with various amusement attractions of many shapes and sizes. From roller coasters to sideshows to everything in between, Atlantic City has been host to some of the wackiest amusements on the east coast.

Today the amusement centers have been toned down significantly from their illustrious past. But thrills and excitement are still around. Two of the four piers in Atlantic City are host to amusement attractions. Additionally, several smaller arcades align the boardwalk. There are some off-property amusement attractions as well, at The Walk and one further inland.

Steel Pier

Virginia Ave & Boardwalk
Atlantic City, NJ
(866) 386-6659

Getting there: Steel Pier is located on the boardwalk, directly across from Trump Taj Mahal.

Steel Pier – the second northernmost pier on the boardwalk – is Atlantic City's answer to the other amusement piers along the shore. It is located directly across from the Trump Taj Mahal and is only accessible from the boardwalk (no parking – travelers by car must park on the street or in a resort). Though not as extensive as the piers in the Wildwoods or Seaside Heights, Steel Pier is a definite must if you are traveling to Atlantic City with a group of youngsters.

Steel Pier first opened during Atlantic City's golden age; in 1898. Since then it has had several ups and downs like everything else in the city. When Donald Trump leased the land from Resorts to complete Trump Taj Mahal, the pier was vacant, and sometimes even used for storage. But when tourism began to rise even more, the Pier found it's way to becoming an amusement center once again, focusing its attention on family entertainment.

Today, the pier has everything you'd expect. Before heading out onto it, you have your choice of many amusement park favorites – cotton candy, funnel cakes, corn dogs, you name it! As you enter (free admission, but pay-per-ride!) you are surrounded by midway games galore. Shoot the water balloon, dunk the basketball, ring toss, and many other favorites are squished into this one small entrance area.

Beyond the games are the rides – Steel Pier has the standard fare – a water flume ride, Tilt-a-Whirl, Ferris Wheel, Go-Carts, and more. No major attractions, but plenty of small ones to satisfy your amusement needs for a few hours.

Crazy Mouse is Steel Pier's claim to a roller coaster. It's the most visible from far away. However, it's not like a typical roller coaster. Think of it as a combination of those spinning teacup-style rides and a traditional track coaster – your coaster's cart spins as you make your way across the twisty track. If you tend to get a little queasy, this ride will definitely make you wish you hadn't eaten that corn dog.

Steel Pier is thin and long, making all the attractions close together – there is not much room on the pier (which also makes it feel very cramped and crowded even though there may not be many people around). By the time you make it to the eastern tip, you have seen it all. But for the real thrill-seekers (or willing sightseers) a quick helicopter ride at the end of the pier is a great experience! It will give you the opportunity to get a perfect view of the Atlantic City skyline, and to take some great aerial photographs.

BOARDWALK AMUSEMENTS

The boardwalk has always been where all the action takes place – and with few exceptions, most of the amusement centers are on the same stretch they've always been. Though nowadays there are considerably less of these nickel-and-dime amusements, they help keep the historic boardwalk atmosphere alive, sometimes year-round.

Located on the site of the world's first successful amusement pier, the **Central Pier Arcade & Speedway** (Tennessee Ave. & Boardwalk, Atlantic City, NJ, 609-345-5219) is in the resort-devoid section of the boardwalk between Sands and Resorts. It is primarily a video arcade with redemption games and "kiddie slots" (slot machines that pay off in souvenir tokens as opposed to coins).

The kiddie slots, though nowhere near as well-kept as their legitimate casino counterparts, offer a special note: they are not actual slot machines, but rather based on the Japanese Pashislo (or "skill-stop") gaming machine. It plays similarly to slot machines, but instead of waiting for the internal chip to stop the spinning, each wheel has a button that allows players to choose exactly when the wheel stops spinning. Skill-stop machines, unlike slot machines, are legal without a casino permit in the state of New Jersey (and most other states in the union). However, the most notable aspect of Central Pier is the large go-cart track way down at the end of the pier.

But historically, Central Pier is particularly special: it is on the site of the world's first successful amusement pier: Applegate's Pier, completed in 1884. Though another amusement pier had been built just three years earlier, it was destroyed in a matter of months due to inadequate infrastructure. However, Applegate's Pier was subdued, offering more of a relaxing experience than the piers that followed or the piers of today.

Between Boardwalk Hall and the Tropicana is the **Playcade Arcade** (2629 Boardwalk, Atlantic City, NJ, http://www.playcade.com). As one of the largest and oldest amusement arcade centers in Atlantic City, Playcade offers diversions of various sorts. They have kiddie slot machines (skill-stops), arcade and video games, redemption games, and more. The indoor facility is open year-round, sometimes until late at night.

Playcade has a wide selection of arcade games despite its smallish space. They have some new releases but mostly established classics. The redemption counter – located at the back of the establishment – has a variety of prizes for those playing redemption games.

In the northern area of the boardwalk, near Resorts, is the **Atlantic City Boardwalk Arcade** (Boardwalk & Ocean Ave, Atlantic City, NJ, 609-345-3710). One of the several amusement centers in the uptown area (including Central Pier and Steel Pier), the Atlantic City Boardwalk Arcade is especially good when it comes to redemption games. It is indoors, and feels a little smaller than other arcades in the area. It has a nice selection of newer video games as well as skill stop-style slot machines.

For a more modern arcade experience, **WOW VR Live!** (New York Avenue & Boardwalk, Atlantic City, NJ), http://www.wowvr.com) is a complete virtual reality experience and video game rolled into one. Participants sit in chairs and wear cumbersome but futuristic virtual reality headgear, and compete one-on-one in virtual world arcade games.

ATLANTIC CITY MINIATURE GOLF

Mississippi Ave & Boardwalk
Atlantic City, NJ
(609) 347-1661

Getting there: On the boardwalk, in Kennedy Plaza, directly across from Atlantic City Boardwalk Hall (at Mississippi Avenue).

Part of (or perhaps immediately next to) Kennedy Plaza is Atlantic City Miniature Golf, which occupies a very unique space. As you stroll down the boardwalk unaware, it will undoubtedly come as an unexpected surprise. It does not fit in with the surrounding environment. But, especially if you're traveling as a family, this is one of the better diversions in Atlantic City.

Located almost immediately across from Boardwalk Hall and next to Kennedy Plaza, Atlantic City Miniature Golf looks almost temporary at first; like artificial golf greens have been laid out onto the boardwalk and could be blown away by a stiff breeze at any time. But this is the beauty of it: instead of transporting you to a Pirate's Cove or other far-off place, it takes advantage of its very unique location. You are golfing on the Atlantic City Boardwalk.

As is to be expected, this is a very popular attraction, so expect some wait especially during the hot summer months. It is a full 18 holes of mini golf, and can take quite a chunk out of your day. But for families or couples, this can be great fun. The course is open during the evening hours as well, and twilight golfing can be especially unique.

The course is not as challenging as other mini-golf courses; this can be a disadvantage if you're a seasoned mini-golfer. But all the basics are there: waterfalls, fountains, and crazy golf greens. But what isn't basic is the beautiful beach and massive Atlantic Ocean – right next to the course. How great!

PASSPORT: VOYAGES OF DISCOVERY

Arctic Ave & Michigan Ave
Atlantic City, NJ
(609) 678-0400

Getting there: At The Walk; the section on the corner of Arctic & Michigan Aves.

One of the real gems of The Walk is an attraction called Passport: Voyages of Discovery. It is a complete entertainment experience that revolves around a motion-simulator ride. Basically this means you will be sitting in a chair and watching a large movie screen as the chair jostles you around in coordination with what's happening onscreen. This is supposed to give you the feeling that you are actually in the movie – it doesn't but its still fun. Passport: Voyages of Discovery is a fairly new chain of motion simulator attractions in the same genre of Ripley's Entertainment. There are locations in Baltimore, Atlantic City, and Niagara Falls.

The ride itself is very similar to Ripley's Moving Theater attraction in places like Niagara Falls. There is one large screen, and several different audience seating "units". The whole room does not move, unlike other virtual reality simulators found in malls across America. Only the seats move. This ruins the illusion of being "in the movie", but not to the point that you won't have a little fun.

Passport: Voyages of Discovery offers a choice of three different "experiences" – which means three different pre-shows and movies, but the same basic principle. The experiences are not designed to be continuously loading. One group must exit before another can enter.

You begin by entering the portal door to the experience of your choice (you have to buy a ticket for a specific one). You (and the others) enter a small theater, which seats around forty people. The show begins with an introductory film about the experience you are about to embark upon. You are told a story to get you in the "mood".

During the introductory film, if the crowd is big enough (and filled with enough children), the host may decide to conduct a mini game show to see who will "captain" the virtual ride. The children will be called up to the front of the room to answer a series of trivia questions – the one with the most correct answers gets special treatment (and the happy knowledge that he or she gets to captain the ride). This show is entirely for kids, but it's well designed and executed.

Next, you are taken into the ride theater, where you are divided into groups to fit into the several seating sections. The screen in front is actually three screens aligned side-by-side. You are seated, the lights dim, and the show begins.

This is one of the longer motion simulator rides you will experience: about twenty minutes! Some of it jostles you around a lot, while other parts almost serve as an educational video (as you learn facts about the environment you are "flying" around). Overall, while not as good as some other rides in places where attractions like this reign supreme (like Orlando), this is definitely a step in the right direction for Atlantic City.

Atlantic City in the Movies

Ocean's Eleven (2001), *Snake Eyes* (1998), *The Pick-Up Artist* (1987), *Sour Grapes* (1998), *The Godfather III* (1990) and of course *Atlantic City* (1980) all featured scenes shot on location in Atlantic City.

STORYBOOK LAND

6415 Black Horse Pike
Egg Harbor Township, NJ
(609) 646-0103

Getting there: Take Black Horse Pike for about 10 miles out of Atlantic City.

Located just outside of Atlantic City, Storybook land is a small, 20-acre theme park catering to families with young children. It is designed with classic children's stories and poems in mind, and throughout the park these stories are represented in various rides and attractions. Despite the small size, however, Storybook Land really packs a lot in.

There is a quality about Storybook Land that makes it a very attractive place to visit – it is not large and noisy like other theme parks, but rather relaxing and extremely homey. The ride selection includes: a small roller coaster, a train ride, an old-time car driving track, and several other small and gentle rides. The property is very grassy and wooded, with plenty of places to relax. Seasonally, Storybook Land has some special events. Around Halloween and Christmas, the park is dressed up for the occasions with special attractions (like a visit from Santa Claus in Christmas and a purposefully-not-scary hayride for Halloween).

Storybook Land has been owned and operated entirely independently since 1955 (it is as old as Disneyland). The yearly operating schedule is generous; they are only closed for about three months out of the year (January through March). During November and December, the park has late afternoon hours on weekends. Ticket prices are reasonable – less than $20 for the 2005 season, and included unlimited rides and attractions for the day. Repeat visitors may be interested in purchasing a season pass.

If you're in the Atlantic City area with small children and want to take them to a very kid-friendly amusement part without a lot of the loud, flashy business found elsewhere, Storybook Land is a great choice.

ENTERTAINMENT AND SPORTS

In addition to the venues within the main resort hotels, Atlantic City boasts several prime locations for shows, entertainment, and sporting events. Some of the places listed here (such as Boardwalk Hall) have historical significance as well as current implementations.

BOARDWALK HALL

2301 Boardwalk
Atlantic City, NJ
(609) 348-7000

Getting there: On the boardwalk, between Tropicana and Trump Plaza.

The Atlantic City Boardwalk Hall was first conceived of in 1910, and eventually manifested into a building for its grand opening on May 31, 1929. Back then it was called the Atlantic City Convention Hall, but since the opening of the newer off-boardwalk convention center in 1997, the original is now referred to as the "Boardwalk Hall". It is located near the southern section of the boardwalk, in between the midtown and downbeach resort areas. Directly on the other side of the convention center is Kennedy Plaza, which hosts seasonal activities such as concerts and mini-golf.

Declared a National Historic Landmark in 1987, the building underwent extensive renovations and restorations, including making better use of the space for various technological innovations that were not available during the building's initial opening. There was an additional renovation in 2001, costing about $90 million, which finally brought the Hall up to par with the best venues around the country.

The building's exterior has a semi-circle shape, with a hard concrete texture. It has that "historic" look which is much different than the surrounding resort-hotels. It has a subdued, classically elegant appeal and lays much lower than the neighboring towers. While entering from the street side is less-than-attractive (you will see various utilitarian entrances and garbage pick-up stations), the boardwalk entrance is grand, and a real step back into the history of Atlantic City architecture.

The Atlantic City Boardwalk Hall has two different venues, which can host a variety of different kinds of events. The main Hall is used for boxing, hockey and other sports, as well as concert events or shows. It is the largest single event center in Atlantic City, which can accommodate over thirteen thousand people. The Hall has hosted Boardwalk Bullies Hockey Club, CardSharks Indoor Football, and the Miss America Pageant. On occasion, neighboring casinos such as Bally's will take advantage of the Adrian Phillips Ballroom, since Bally's does not have a large venue of its own. The well-known SMG management company, headquartered in Philadelphia, manages the entire venue.

Boardwalk Hall can be host to several different kinds of sporting events. Atlantic City's East Coast Hockey League (ECHL) team, The Boardwalk Bullies, considers the hall its home arena. The season runs standard for minor league hockey, starting around late October. Also, brand new in the spring of 2004, is the inaugural season of New Jersey's only professional indoor football team, the Atlantic City CardSharks.

In addition, the Ultimate Fighting Championship holds occasional events here, as well as professional boxing matches, and countless concert tours. As it is the largest venue in Atlantic City, many big names are drawn to the hall. If you are interested in visiting or would like to know about a specific event, you can inquire by contacting Boardwalk Hall's box office, or online at Ticketmaster.

THE MISS AMERICA ORGANIZATION

Headquarters:
2 Miss America Way, Suite 1000
Atlantic City, NJ
(609) 345-7571

By far the most famous event to take place on a regular basis at Boardwalk Hall is the annual Miss America Pageant. The finals of the competition are broadcast live at Boardwalk Hall from coast to coast. In terms of nationwide publicity, this event is number one for Atlantic City. As a result, this pageant is milked and milked all over the city until the udder of market saturation is dry. You will notice the street name "One Miss America Way", countless signs and Billboards touting this event. And in the weeks leading up to the finals, the city dresses up.

The Miss America Organization is officially a scholarship competition for women between the ages of 17 and 24. The organization gives out about $45 million annually in scholarship and assistance money. Though scholarships are awarded at various levels of the competition (not just in the finals), the actual title of "Miss America" is bestowed onto one woman each year. Being Miss America is actually a job unto itself – it requires traveling many miles throughout the year-long tenure, to support various other organizations and worthy causes.

The first Miss America was Margaret Gorman of Washington, DC, who was crowned in 1921, and after that there was a competition every year until 1927. But when the Great Depression hit, the pageant went into hiatus for several years, while Boardwalk Hall was constructed. The first depression-era pageant was held in 1933, the first in Boardwalk Hall. Since then, there have been a few years that lacked a Miss America, but 2003 was the 75th crowning, and the Miss America Pageant is going strong year after year.

There is an elaborate history and aura to the Miss America Organization and competition, which is beyond the scope of this guide. It is not just an annual event that draws nationwide attention, but has on many occasions been directly affected by various national movements (both positively and negatively). The controversial aspects of the competition are extensive, and much information is available through research. The competition is endlessly imitated since the organization's recipe calls for almost certain success.

But this is not a political book. Atlantic City takes great pride in its hosting of Miss America. It is an ideal location for the competition as well, especially since the dawn of the casino era. It is an integral aspect to Atlantic City history and tourism, and one of the few remnants of Atlantic City's past that still remains nearly intact today.

Kennedy Plaza

Georgia Avenue & Boardwalk
Atlantic City, NJ

Getting there: On the boardwalk, directly across from Boardwalk Hall.

Directly across from the Atlantic City Boardwalk Hall is Kennedy Plaza, which is, among other things, a restful showcase and stage, and an outdoor garden. The plaza fits in well with its Boardwalk Hall counterpart on the opposite side of the boardwalk. It is partitioned from the beach with a large stone structure, complete with evenly spaced pedestals. As with the Hall itself, it feels very structurally permanent, with well-groomed and maintained stone décor. Although accessible and open free to the public year-round, it is particularly stunning during the summertime, when the flowers and plants within the garden are at their peak of color.

In the center of the plaza is a statue of a worker. The large stone plaque next to it is dedicated to people that passed away while working on Atlantic City's redevelopment since 1979. The statue was erected on April 28, 1998 and serves as a centerpiece for the plaza. Beyond the statue, against the far back of Kennedy Plaza, is a bust of John F. Kennedy himself.

Of particular note to perform on stage at Kennedy Plaza is the Chicken Bone Beach Jazz Concert Series. Every summer on a weekly schedule, groups sponsored by the Chicken Bone Beach society perform at the plaza to commemorate African-American heritage in Atlantic

City. Chicken Bone Beach – the unofficially dubbed strip of beachfront south of Missouri Avenue – was where African-American families wishing to vacation in Atlantic City were restricted between the 1900s and the 1950s.

SKATE ZONE

501 North Albany Avenue
Atlantic City, NJ
(609) 441-1780

Getting There: Take Black Horse Pike (Albany Avenue) out of Atlantic City. Next to Bader Field.

The Philadelphia Flyers Skate Zone is a chain of family-friendly indoor ice skating facilities owned by Comcast-Spectacor (parent company of the Philadelphia Flyers as well as other sport teams and venues). Headquartered in Philadelphia, they operate area facilities in several locations, including Voorhees, Bethlehem, Pennsauken, and Atlantic City.

The Atlantic City facility opened in 1999, and caters to local interests. Several clubs and local groups make use of the indoor rink, which is open nearly year-round. Groups that use the facility include: Atlantic City Jr. Bullies Hockey Club, Atlantic City Figure Skating Club, Flyer's Youth Hockey League, Old Men's Hockey League, and several others. There is also almost always daily rink time (call for schedule) devoted to free skating, and is open to the public.

The facility is equipped to rent skates, as well as a pro shop ("Pro Zone"), a small arcade, a snack bar ("Snack Zone"), and, of course an ice rink with an audience capacity of about 300.

SANDCASTLE BASEBALL STADIUM

545 North Albany Avenue
Atlantic City, NJ
Tickets: (609) 344-SURF

Getting There: Take Black Horse Pike (Albany Avenue) out of Atlantic City. Next to Bader Field.

The Atlantic City Surf, a team in the minor league Atlantic League of Professional Baseball (ALPB). Their home ballpark is Sandcastle Baseball stadium, right next to Flyers Skate Zone on Albany Avenue.

Sandcastle Stadium is angled perfectly for a great view of Atlantic City while in the bleachers: the baseball diamond in the foreground, and the Atlantic City skyline way in the distance. The stadium seats 5,900 spectators at capacity. Public admission to the facility is limited to sporting events; tours are generally not available.

Admission tickets for home games of the Atlantic City Surf can be purchased at The Sandcastle, or through the team's website. Seating choices include a variety of levels, from standard seats to deluxe and premium box seats.

GOLF COURSES

Golfing is a big deal on the Jersey Shore, and the area is peppered with golf courses with different sizes and abilities. Although no professional courses are directly within Atlantic City, a short drive inland can be fruitful for anybody wishing to enjoy a day on one of the area's courses.

Many of the golf courses in the area are private and membership may be available by invitation only. However, public courses are also available. Pay-per-day rates for these facilities can cost around $60-$100, depending on when in the week, or what time of day you wish to golf. Following is a select list of public golf courses.

Blue Heron Pines Golf Club (550 West Country Club Drive, Cologne, NJ, 609-965-1800, http://www.blueheronpines.com) is a pay-per-game facility that offers two completely different 18-hole courses to choose from. Frequent golfers can also enjoy various levels of membership that allow course access on a more regular basis. On occasion, golf packages may be available with select area resorts and hotels.

The Empire Golf Management is responsible for the daily management of several courses around the greater Atlantic City area. One of their public courses in particular, the **Twisted Dune Golf Club** (2101 Ocean Height Avenue, Egg Harbor Township, NJ, 609-653-8019, http://www.twisteddune.com) offers 18 holes of various ratings, as well as practice and teaching facilities.

Harbor Pines Golf Club (500 St. Andrews Drive, Egg Harbor Township, NJ, 609-927-0006, http://www.harborpines.com) is a pay-per-day 18-hole golf course, which also features a collection of on-site homes in gated community style, called "Harbor Pine Estates". The course's clubhouse is particularly large and well-appointed. Of course, membership options are also available for frequent golf enthusiasts.

For a more all-encompassing golf outing, **Seaview Resort and Spa** by Marriott (401 South New York Road, Galloway Township, NJ, 609-652-1800, http://www.seaviewgolf.com) is a complete resort complex that has all kinds of activities, as well as two full 18-hole golf courses. Though it particularly caters to golfers, the resort has tennis courts, indoor and outdoor pools, business meeting space, an on-site restaurant, and a full health club. Additionally, the **Renault Winery** Resort has a full golf course on the site of its vineyard, as well as hotel accommodations, restaurants, and more (see the Renault Winery section for more details).

If you wish to experience a private country club but without all the fees involved, the **Atlantic City Country Club** is open only to those guests staying in an area resort owned by Caesars Entertainment (either Bally's, Caesars, or the Atlantic City Hilton). For more information about this golf experience, contact the Caesars Entertainment resort you wish to stay at prior to booking.

MUSEUMS AND CULTURE

In 2004, Atlantic City celebrated its 150th anniversary. Though the attractions and culture have changed dramatically since 1854, it is a history still alive today in many of the area's attractions, the city's structure and commerce. Visitors will appreciate today's attractions and development all the more with an understanding of the city's past. Over time, many important historical figures have graced the beaches and boardwalk, each leaving their mark. Many firsts, many oddities, and many corporate trials found their way to this spot on the coast. Visitors are often amazed to learn that there is much more to Atlantic City's value than beach resort casinos. As a testament to its long and winding history, the Atlantic City of today is host to many cultural options, from museums to monuments and memorials. Some attractions are preserved relics from the past, while others are newer additions to a constantly expanding city. The attractions listed here are located both on and off the boardwalk.

Atlantic City's Historic Places

The **National Register of Historic Places** (http://www.ns.nps.gov) lists 12 entries in Atlantic City proper. Among the historic sites: the **Absecon Lighthouse** (added to the register in 1971), **Boardwalk Hall** (added in 1987), and **Madison Hotel** (added in 1984).

ATLANTIC CITY HISTORICAL MUSEUM AND ART CENTER

New Jersey Ave & Boardwalk
Atlantic City, NJ
Art Center: (609) 347-5839

Getting There: Located on Garden Pier, just north of Showboat.

Historically, Garden Pier has always been the calmest pier in Atlantic City. When it first opened to the public in 1913, it was an outdoor theater, decorated with ornate flowers and plants. If you were looking for an afternoon of cultural refinement and sun, your only option in Atlantic City was the Garden Pier.

This is also true today. As the northernmost pier, it is located immediately across from the largely undeveloped lot just north of Showboat. The surrounding area is barren and uninviting, but the Garden Pier is a definite cultural highlight of the city. It is host to two distinct buildings. The Art Center is to the left as you enter the Pier's steel gate, and the Historical Museum is on the right.

The Atlantic City Historical Museum (609-347-5839, http://www.acmuseum.org) features comprehensive displays highlighting important moments in Atlantic City history. The museum is a small room, but in fact jam-packed with articles and information. The museum is a great start to Atlantic City's first 100 years. It features a permanent exhibit, called "Atlantic City, Playground of the Nation" with all kinds of memorabilia such as souvenirs, photos, clothes, and posters. Visitors can learn about the boardwalk, the many amusement piers that have come and gone, and the political and corporate giants (such as H.J Heinz and George Tilyou) that have graced the city. Of particular note is the wide array of Miss America-related articles.

The museum also showcases a documentary on Atlantic City history, called "Boardwalk Ballyhoo: The Magic of Atlantic City". Copies of the documentary can be purchased at the small gift stand at the entrance to the museum. The stand also sells some very informative historical books, and some unique gift items. On occasion, the museum houses temporary exhibits.

Next door to the museum is the **Atlantic City Art Center** (609-347-5837). Though not focused on historical interests, it houses three galleries featuring a rotating schedule of art exhibits. Overall, the Atlantic City Cultural Center on Garden Pier is a definite must-see for any first time visitor to Atlantic City.

THE NEW JERSEY KOREAN WAR MEMORIAL

Brighton Park & Boardwalk
Atlantic City, NJ

Getting There: On the boardwalk, between Bally's Park Place and Brighton Park.

Almost exactly where Park Place meets the boardwalk, sandwiched between Brighton Park and Bally's Park Place, is the New Jersey Korean War Memorial. It is accessible immediately off the boardwalk. As you enter the small enclave, you first notice two distinct walls, one made of granite and etched with names of servicemen who died during the Korean War, and one of sand-colored stone, with reliefs of American soldiers charging out of it. A statue in the center is of a single soldier, with his helmet off, holding onto several ID tags. In warmer weather, water cascades down from the memorial wall.

This is a totally free outdoor memorial dedicated to those who fought in the Korean War. Around 250 people attended the groundbreaking on March 14, 2000, and it opened to the public on November 13 that same year. It is a touching tribute to those who served; those who returned, and those who did not.

CIVIL RIGHTS GARDEN

Getting There: Located immediately next to the Carnegie Library Center (part of the Richard Stockton College of New Jersey).

The Civil Rights Garden is a small garden with a winding walkway, a reflecting pool, and statues that seem to burst through the ground. Each of these statues has inscriptions of important people and places in the history of Civil Rights. In the center of the garden is a large bell (similar to the Liberty Bell), which rings during special occasions.

The garden features a nice landscape of flowers and plants (particularly in the summertime). Though it feels peaceful, there is definitely a feeling of gravity as you pass through the garden's gates. A wrought iron fence encapsulates the many pedestals. Visitors guide themselves along the path, stopping at the pedestals to read the inscriptions.

RIPLEY'S *BELIEVE IT OR NOT!* MUSEUM

New York Ave & Boardwalk
Atlantic City, NJ
(609) 347-2001

Getting There: On the boardwalk, across from Central Pier.

Let's face it – the invention of the wax museum is the single greatest accomplishment of western civilization. And wherever there is a vacation town, there seems to be a **Ripley's** *Believe it or Not!* **Museum**. If you are driving towards a town with billboards for mini-golf, go-carts or roller coasters, and fudge shop after fudge shop, chances are you'll see a Ripley's. Atlantic City, Niagara Falls, Myrtle Beach, Wisconsin Dells, and many other towns have this attraction.

The Ripley's museum in Atlantic City is located directly on the boardwalk by the ocean, sandwiched in between two large resort-hotels. It is just south of the Trump Taj Mahal, in a two story high building designed to look like it has just been whacked with a colorful wrecking ball, which has been decorated to look like Earth. The exhibits inside include a replica of the Jersey Devil skeleton, as well as some classic Ripley "artifacts" such as shrunken heads and unusually talented contortionists, and people who smoke cigarettes through their eyes.

Robert Leroy Ripley was born in 1890 in Santa Rosa, California. In 1908, he sold his first comic to LIFE magazine. After working for the San Francisco Chronicle and Boston's "The Globe", he decided to travel abroad. In 1918, he draws a cartoon featuring sports oddities, and one year later draws a comic called "Believe It Or Not!" From then on, Ripley traveled the world in search of oddities to write about and publish in his comic strips. In 1929 his strips earned syndication, read by millions worldwide. Ripley would work for radio, create short films and explore different avenues for his "Believe It or Not!" idea. In 1933, the first "Odditorium" museum opened in Chicago, followed shortly thereafter by San Diego and Dallas. In 1939 there was even an Odditorium opening in Times Square in New York City. In 1949, Robert Ripley collapsed on the set of his television show, and died shortly thereafter. The first Odditorium to open its doors in Atlantic City was in 1954 – but it closed in 1957.

Unlike many non-resort attractions, Ripley's *Believe It or Not!* Museum is open year-round, so even in the dead of winter you can walk through and enjoy the wonders. The entire museum tour is self-guided, and you can go through it in as little as half an hour, but you can take as long as you wish.

DR. JONATHON PITNEY HOUSE

57 Shore Road
Absecon, NJ
(609) 569-1799

Getting there: Route 157 (off US Route 9), right on Church Street in Absecon, corner of Shore Road.

Before there was a resort town, and well before there were casinos, there was lonely Absecon Island, nothing more than a vast marshland surrounding a tiny village. Around 1820, after Dr. Jonathon Pitney graduated from medical school in New York, he made his way to the village, and set up his home there.

But Pitney had a dream. He envisioned a resort community on the Island, and a "Railroad to Nowhere" which would bring visitors from nearby towns into this would-be vacation paradise. It was Dr. Pitney's direct involvement in the establishment of a railway system to this city by the Atlantic Ocean (ultimately dubbed "Atlantic City" by the railroad company), which earned him the title "The Father of Atlantic City".

Pitney's house was originally built in 1799, and another wing was built (by Pitney himself) in 1848. In 1997, the house was restored and added to the National Register of Historic Places the following year. Today it occasionally functions as both a historical site and bed-and-breakfast.

Visitors may tour the Dr. Jonathon Pitney House in Absecon City (just off Absecon Island), or spend one or more nights in one of their especially romantic and classically-appointed rooms and suites. The house and property are colonial in style, and guests are pampered with homemade breakfasts, as well as afternoon tea. The house is ideally suited for romance. Packages are available, if you are interested in a romantic getaway.

ABSECON LIGHTHOUSE

31 South Rhode Island Ave
Atlantic City, NJ
(609) 449-1360

Getting There: North of Showboat, drive west on Rhode Island Avenue, until you reach the lighthouse.

Nestled in between otherwise unimpressive buildings, in a mostly residential area of Atlantic City, is the tallest lighthouse in New Jersey (and the third tallest in the United States). At 171 feet, the Absecon Lighthouse played an integral part in the development of the city, and of the Jersey Shore in general. It has recently been totally renovated and today serves as a hot historical attraction. The Absecon Lighthouse is named for the island on which it is situated, and is also one of the oldest structures in Atlantic City, built well before the boardwalk.

Dr. Jonathon Pitney, considered by many to be the father of Atlantic City, cited numerous nautical disasters in Absecon Beach (the "Graveyard Inlet") as a reason to build a lighthouse. In 1854 the money was secured. Three years later, on January 15, 1857, the lighthouse was first lit. For years it helped seagoing vessels avoid the treachery of Absecon Beach. In 1933 the light was extinguished, and for a while the structure remained largely unused, except for some ceremonial events and mild tourism. In 1971, the lighthouse was placed on the National Register of Historic Places. After years of restorations and reorganizations, the tower itself finally opened to the public in 1999.

The Absecon Lighthouse is visible in the near distance from the northern end of the boardwalk, particularly north of Showboat. Visitors may explore the gift shop, or climb the 228 steps to the viewing platform just below the lantern room. Though it is within walking distance of the boardwalk, it is farther away than it seems, and you will probably enjoy it better by taking a short car or taxi ride, especially if you anticipate climbing to the top.

As east coasters, and New Englanders particularly, are well aware, lighthouses are big deals, both for tourism and for historical reasons. Absecon Lighthouse is among the best; but for those interested, a drive to the southern tip of New Jersey brings you to the Cape May Lighthouse, and a short drive north will bring you to the Barnegat Lighthouse. Together, these three sister lighthouses are among the most important in New Jersey. Today the Inlet Public/Private Association (IPPA) operates them.

LUCY THE ELEPHANT

9200 Atlantic Avenue
Margate, NJ
(609) 823-6473

Getting there: Take Atlantic Avenue south of Atlantic City several miles. It will appear on your left. Limited parking is available.

For those not familiar with the eclectic history of the Jersey Shore, Lucy the Elephant is an odd thing to explain. Given the many other monstrous and goofy architectural feats of today, Lucy may not be the most impressive thing ever built. But it has a certain quality that captures the history of the area quite well.

Lucy is not in Atlantic City. Rather, the attraction is two miles south in the town of Margate. Though you can walk there (at least an hour one-way from the Atlantic City Hilton), you will have to maneuver through the streets since the boardwalk does not go that far south. You will probably be better off driving or taking public transportation. But, if only for the sake of a mild thrill, this is definitely a hyped and must-see attraction, especially if you're traveling with young people or curio connoisseurs

So who is Lucy? She is a six-story tall elephant-shaped building (the largest "elephant" in the world). She is the quintessential roadside attraction: something totally pointless and somehow irresistible. She was initially built in 1881 as an attempt to sell real estate in the area (it has even been said that she was the area's first tourist attraction). She has been a real estate office, a summer home, a tavern, and a derelict landmark. In 1976, she was added to the National Register of Historic Places. The attraction is small, quaint and clean.

Driving to Lucy from Atlantic City is simple: just take Atlantic Avenue south until you reach her. However, Atlantic Avenue is very stop-and-go so expect the four miles to take about fifteen minutes or more. As you approach, the elephant really stands out from the rest of the area. Aside from its size, it looks obviously artificial, like a papier-mâché creation, but that's the point. The parking is limited, but don't worry – you don't need to spend much time here to really enjoy it. Just check out the small museum, buy some gifts from the shop, and hop back in the car. The parking spaces for Lucy would be prime for beach-goers, but parking there is not allowed, unless you buy a tour ticket.

There is something totally adorable about Lucy the Elephant. She may very well be this area's very first roadside attraction, and has stood the test of time, even by Atlantic City standards. The exhibits inside highlight the history of this creation, with photographs, diagrams and a video presentation. The whole package is very kitschy and cute. Tours are guided, although the attraction itself is small and self-contained enough that it really doesn't need to be. She was actually modeled to look like an Indian elephant, which accounts for the carriage on her back. Also, despite the fact that she has a woman's name, she has tusks and is therefore not female.

The inside of Lucy is unexpected. As the tour begins, you climb up one of her hind legs in a narrow, winding staircase (like that of a lighthouse), and end up in a large room, reminiscent of a turn-of-the-century courthouse. You are in Lucy's torso - there is fine oak paneling and wood flooring, and everything is clean and tidy. There are small exhibits around the outer edge of this room. In this main room, you will watch a short video on the history of Lucy; her purpose and development. Then your guide will take you up on another staircase to the very top of Lucy where there is a truly great view of the beach and of surrounding Margate.

The tour is short; don't expect it to take longer than about 20 minutes (and the video takes up most of that time). If you're looking to kill an entire day, this attraction won't do it. But if you're anywhere around, this is honest, historical Jersey Shore tack that is sure to please anybody. Additionally, Lucy is a seasonal attraction, with limited hours during off-peak times of year.

The Distant City

Lucy is a walk from the casinos, but if you head out onto the beach, which is right next to Lucy, you can see in the distance the entire Atlantic City skyline. Of course, the boardwalk doesn't stretch this far south, and in the summer this section of the beach is crowded with swimming Jersey Shore vacationers.

Margate's atmosphere is surprisingly different from Atlantic City. It is much quieter, more relaxed, and very few buildings are more than 3-4 stories high. Aligning the beach are residences, not casinos. People carry towels and beach blankets, not full shopping bags and empty wallets.

OCEAN LIFE CENTER

800 North New Hampshire Ave
Atlantic City, NJ
(609) 348-2880

Getting there: Going north on Atlantic Avenue, turn left on New Hampshire Avenue, and drive to the end of the road.

The resident aquarium in Atlantic City is the **Ocean Life Center**. Located in the Historic Gardner's Basin, the center features as many as eleven large tanks filled with various species of ocean life. There is even a special tank that allows visitors to reach in and touch some of the more unusual and exotic (but safe) animals.

The tanks of the aquarium each specialize in a particular kind of ocean environment. The "Fish of the New Jersey Coast" tank contains bluegill, weakfish, kingfish, nurse sharks, and more. The "Coral Reef" tank has varieties of sea life that live in a reef environment. Other tanks include "Seahorses & Shellfish", "Tropical Beauties", "Live Moon Jelly Fish", and more. The Center's inhabitants tend to rotate a bit due to species' availability. "Sea Sights & Sounds", "A Ships Bridge", and other permanent exhibits, as well as computer terminals loaded with marine life information, make for a well-rounded experience.

The Center is rather small, but packed with things to see and do. It consists of three floors, the main floor being the main aquarium area. Most of the exhibits are visible right from the front desk, which is also a gift shop. The second floor consists mainly of interactive exhibits and sets. The top floor – the roof of the center – has an outdoor portion that offers visitors a great 365-degree view of the Basin, the Marina District, and even the distant boardwalk skyline.

The Ocean Life Center first opened in 1999. Access by car is the most convenient. It is located near the tip of the Gardner's Basin, surrounded almost completely by water. Directly on the other side of the water is the Trump Marina resort and the Farley State Marina.

BALIC WINERY

6623 Harding Highway (US Route 40)
Mays Landing, NJ
(609) 625-2166

Getting there: Take US Route 40 (Black Horse Pike / Albany Avenue) out of Atlantic City. Stay on Route 40 through Mays Landing and towards Buena.

Mays Landing has had the winery in some form since the turn of the 19th century, but wine entrepreneur Savo Balic purchased the land in 1966, renaming it the **Balic Winery**. At 57 acres, Balic Winery today bottles about 12,000 cases of wine per year, at 6-12 bottles per case, one bottle at a time. The processing center on the property itself caters mostly to the sales of wine and wine tasting.

Tours are available; just ask for one. Visitors will note that Balic Winery is a functional facility and does not as much cater to tourists as do other vineyards in the area, such as Renault Winery. If you are interested in wine, however, and want a quick vineyard experience, Balic Winery is a good choice. For a more elaborate daytrip or weekend trip, Renault offers a more comprehensive package.

RENAULT WINERY

72 Bremen Avenue
Egg Harbor City, NJ
(609) 965-2111

Getting there: Take US Route 30 from Atlantic City West to Bremen Avenue (about 16 miles – a large wine bottle serves as a landmark for the turn). Turn right and drive about 2 miles.

Located in the New Jersey Pine Barrens about 35 miles away from Atlantic City, the **Renault Winery** complex can be an entire vacation destination in and of itself. The property features a hotel, several restaurants, a golf course, and a vineyard complete with comprehensive tour and wine tasting. Ample space is available for weddings and conferences.

Louis Nicholas Renault first purchased the land on which the winery sits in 1864. After having some bad luck with his vineyards in France and California, he moved his operation to Egg Harbor and proceeded to win many awards for the wine produced there. During Prohibition, the winery was sold to John D'Agostino who sold wine on a limited basis. Since then it has exchanged hands several times, until Joseph P. Milza, who currently owns and operates the entire resort, finally acquired it.

Stepping onto the main vineyard complex today feels very much like stepping into a small French vineyard. The **House of Renault** is the centerpiece of the winery, made of dark wood and surrounded by a French-influenced garden. The entry doors for the main tour are massive wooden structures. The small garden surrounding the house has a few gazebos for relaxing and gathering, and a stream of water flows throughout, with walking bridges crossing it in places. There is also a gift shop on the site as well as a place to buy Renault wine. The guided tour focuses on the wine processing, and includes history of the vineyard ("how could such a vineyard have wound up in Egg Harbor Township?"). Your tour guide will bring you into the real working rooms in the various stages of grape harvesting, fermentation, and distribution. At the end of the tour, Renault gives you the opportunity to taste some select wines.

The **Renault Gourmet Restaurant** has been touted as one of the most romantic places to eat in the Atlantic City area. Across the complex is the **Tuscany House**, a small hotel that caters to guests of the vineyard and nearby golf course. The rooms, like the rest of the resort, are reminiscent of fine European styles. Inside is **Joseph's Restaurant**, which offers classy décor and a diverse menu.

The **Vineyard Golf** is a brand new addition to the Renault complex, opened in 2004, which really transforms the complex from just a hotel and vineyard to a complete vacation resort. This unique course offers on some holes a very nice view of the vast vineyard property. The course is full-size, covering about 7,000 yards on the complex. They offer memberships as well as a tee-at-a-time option.

Guests wishing to make Renault their destination of choice have the option of several vacation packages that may include rooms, vineyard tours, gourmet dinners, and golf tee times. Call the main Renault Winery number for more information. This is definitely a must-see attraction in south Jersey. It is family-friendly for a vineyard, but there isn't much to do for those not into wine, golf, or fine dining. At one point the Renault Winery was the largest producer of wine in the United States, and it remains one of the oldest operating vineyards in the country today.

THE NOYES MUSEUM

Lily Lake Road
Oceanville, NJ
(609) 652-8848

Getting there: Take U.S. 30 / White Horse Pike out of Atlantic City, and north onto U.S. 9 for about 4 miles. Right on Lily Lake Road.

Entrepreneurs Fred and Ethel Noyes had first hoped to open a fine art museum in south Jersey as early as 1974, when their sale of the History Towne of Smithville to ABC provided enough money to start preplanning. After Mrs. Noyes death in 1979, the museum's future rested on the shoulders of the Mr. and Mrs. Fred Winslow Noyes foundation. The museum finally opened in 1983.

The Noyes Museum is directly adjacent to the Edgar B. Forsythe National Wildlife Refuge, in an idyllic location. It is a small museum, but full; it focuses primarily on folk art and craft (art created with practical purpose), particularly American art. The museum has a permanent collection as well as temporary exhibits. Among other exhibits, it has a large collection of hunting decoys as well as a selection of cottage arts, such as quilts, woodworking, and pottery. There is also a special section dedicated to art on display from local schools.

The museum also has a shop on the premises, where you can purchase collectible art and other exhibit-related memorabilia. There is also adequate space for corporate or private functions. Membership options are also available.

PARKS AND RECREATION

The Jersey Shore is host to a wide variety of outdoor activities. However, most other shore points revolve around swimming or summertime activities. Atlantic City is unique in this aspect – it has sports and recreational activities of all sorts, which range from the standard summertime fare to truly unique retreats and even wildlife experiences and education centers.

In addition to opportunities within the city, some significant natural and recreational activities are a short drive away from the city. State and Federal parks are abundant in New Jersey, and two of the most important ones are located just outside Atlantic City.

EDWIN B. FORSYTHE NATIONAL WILDLIFE REFUGE

Great Creek Road
Oceanville, NJ
(609) 652-1665

Getting There: US Route 9 north out of Atlantic City takes you past the western edge of much of the refuge. Great Creek Road in Oceanville takes you to the main headquarters.

Much of the Jersey Shore (particularly the south Shore) is uninhabitable marsh. For this reason, arriving at various Shore points, including Atlantic City, requires first traversing large land masses of flat, marshy landscape and shallow lakes. Only the very edges – just along the ocean – have been developed.

The Edwin B. Forsythe National Wildlife Refuge is about 40,000 acres representative of this type of coastal wetlands landscape. The refuge is largely inaccessible; however, there is an 8-mile expansive donation-funded vehicle "safari" within the area that gives a good impression of the land. The refuge serves mainly as a resting place for migratory birds (like portions of New York City's Gateway National Recreation Area). If you are a bird watcher, you will feel particularly at home here. There are "patches" of the reserve located at strategic points just north of Atlantic City. The main vehicular entrance is accessible via Route 9 Just north of Atlantic City (take White Horse Pike to 9 North).

The Refuge is part of the New Jersey Coastal Heritage Trail. This series of parks and natural environments runs down the Jersey Shore from Sandy Hook to Cape May, and then wraps a little bit around the southern tip of the state. It is meant to be a trail for vehicles to follow down the shore. The trail itself is not one particular "thing", but rather a collection of independent federal and state run sites that have been grouped in this manner. In other words, if you are driving down the Jersey Shore, you are exploring the Coastal Heritage Trail.

WHARTON STATE FOREST AND BATSTO VILLAGE

4110 Nesco Road
Hammonton, NJ
Main Office: (609) 561-0024
Batsto: (609) 561-3262

Getting there: Exit 50 north off the Garden State Parkway to US 9, follow signs to Batsto Village (via 542 west).

Wharton State Forest, approximately twenty miles away from Atlantic City, is the largest state forest in New Jersey. It is not directly on the Jersey Shore (unlike the Edwin B. Forsythe National Wildlife Refuge), but it is close and is a stark contrast to the Shore's natural landscape. Consisting of about 110,000 acres, Wharton covers ground in three counties: Burlington, Camden, and Atlantic. It was named after Joseph Wharton, who purchased large portions of land in the area during the late 1800s, with the intent to reap financial benefits by using the land for its agriculture and commercial assets. But Wharton passed away before any real damage to the forest was done. New Jersey purchased the land in the mid-1950s, and today the New Jersey Division of Parks and Forestry manages it. Officially, Wharton State Forest is part of the New Jersey Pinelands area.

Driving into Wharton State Forest, especially from the heavily populated Jersey Shore area, with eight-or-more-lane highways, seems like an unusual and sudden jolt. In a matter of feet, the road changes from a massive highway to a mere 2-lane country road, deeply shrouded by tall trees on either side. Signs from the Garden State Parkway and Atlantic City Expressway point to the appropriate exit to reach the forest, but don't expect it to be right around the corner.

Though most of the forest remains in its natural state, some areas within it have been developed both recreationally and commercially. There are year-round campsites scattered all around the area, particularly near Crowley Landing, Atsion, and Batsto Village. Route 542 and 206 are the two main thruways into and out of Wharton, but there are dozens of unpaved roads that take you as far into the forest as you are willing to go. There are hiking trails, natural picnic and swimming areas, and horseback riding trails.

The most significant of these is Batsto Village, the principal purchase of Joseph Wharton, made in 1876. Originally, however, Charles Read created Batsto Iron Works on the Batsto River in 1766. It changed hands several times since then (eventually landing on Wharton), while always maintaining its industrial iron-and-glassmaking core. Today the buildings are preserved, and visitors are free to explore the village on foot and even walk into several dozen buildings to learn about the industry of the day. Visitors will notice the buildings in Batsto Village have a historic cabin look to them. The bridge over Batsto Lake offers a great view of the small, serene lake.

If you are interested in seeing Batsto Village but want to get a taste of Wharton State Forest along the way, 542 off the Garden State Parkway (going north, take exit 50 north to 542) will take you along the southern edge of the forest, a very wooded drive, and past the water at Crowley Landing, where recreational boating is allowed.

BEL HAVEN CANOES AND KAYAKS

1227 Route 542
Green Bank, NJ
(609) 965–2205

Getting there: North on Garden State Parkway to exit 50 (US Route 9 north) take exit to 542 west (follow signs to Batsto Village). Take for about 8 miles.

For the athletic nature lover, the New Jersey Pinelands area offers outdoor water canoeing and kayaking activities close to Atlantic City. Bel Haven, in the Wharton State Forest area, offers options for adventurous souls such as canoeing, kayaking and more. Explore the Oswego, Mullica, Wading, or Batsto rivers either in large groups or by yourself. You and your group are generally free to explore the river on your own, and you may even stop at various points to explore. The rivers are generally calm, though there may be some rougher sections on occasion.

Prices are per canoe per day, but tours can run anywhere from a few hours to several days (nearby campsites are available along the various river routes). This activity requires a certain amount of athletic ability and a basic knowledge of canoeing or kayaking. However, on occasion, guided tours may be available for certain routes and seasons. Canoes are advised for two people, whereas kayaks are suitable for one.

According to the **New Jersey Division of Parks and Forestry,** New Jersey has 39 state parks, 11 state forests, and 3 state recreational facilities.

HISTORIC GARDNER'S BASIN

New Hampshire Ave & Parkside Ave
Atlantic City, NJ

Getting there: Take Atlantic or Pacific Avenue to New Hampshire Avenue, then take a left.

Tucked away in a small corner of Atlantic City that seems out of the way from everything else, is historic Gardner's Basin. Modeled after a New England fishing village, this small, gated area is a real unexpected and pleasant surprise. Most people traveling there are destined for either one of several privately-owned Atlantic City cruises, or the family-friendly Ocean Life Center, but the entire area is a real treat and features several different unique opportunities (and one heck of a nice view). And better yet, most of these attractions, even the boating excursions, can be open year round (but call ahead during the winter months).

Gardner's Basin is located on a small peninsula immediately across from Trump Marina. It is near the northern end of the boardwalk (after it wraps around Absecon Island, north of Showboat). Enter the area by car via New Hampshire Avenue. The Basin, named after former Atlantic City Mayor John H. Gardner, was actually the location of the first hotels in Atlantic City. A majority of the surrounding water area is devoted to various marinas - some of which have vessels that operate public tours and charters.

The area has had its ups and downs over the years, much like the rest of Atlantic City. However, the recent renovation of Gardner's Basin allowed for the new Ocean Life Center, as well as several major renovations to the area. Now visitors can eat lunch, take a boat cruise, explore oceanography, or just walk around this unique village. You may see people fishing off one of the three shores of the peninsula, or snap some photos of the Marina District, or just-over-the-bridge Brigantine.

Gardner's Basin is a small but pretty area, scattered with fishing-village-style buildings. They look very much like small country houses that have been converted into even smaller restaurants, bars, or shops. Parking (and limited boat docking) is free to visitors, so feel free to walk around a little bit.

From the main parking lot, the first establishment you'll notice is the **Back Bay Ale House** (609-449-0006). The exterior looks small, and when you look inside, the interior is even smaller. A small bar mostly takes up the main area, but food is served both inside and on a patio outside. Also nearby is **Back Bay Ice Cream**, which serves all the classic cold treats, including snacks and gelato.

The **Flying Cloud Café** (609-345-8222) has a great waterfront location, where you can enjoy a nice selection of specialty seafood dishes, including a raw bar. The **Lobster Shanty** (609-344-9030), with a great view of the Gardner's Basin marina, allows you to dine on lobster whilst you watch boats move in and of the area.

All restaurants in the Gardner's Basin area are quick eats and very casual. The hours vary seasonally and by establishment so it's a good idea to check ahead of time by calling (although no reservations are required). Expect lots of Atlantic City locals as well as tourists. Children are welcome here, and it can be especially rewarding after an afternoon of exploring the Ocean Life Center.

BOAT CRUISES AND CHARTERS

New Hampshire Ave & Parkside Ave
Atlantic City, NJ

Getting there: Boats depart from Historic Gardner's Basin. Take Atlantic or Pacific Avenue north and take a left at New Hampshire Avenue.

If boating is your thing, there is an entire culture in New Jersey devoted to the boating industry. Marinas are abundant all down the Jersey Shore (its a very big business) and both pleasure and commercial boaters make use of the various facilities. As a result, there is much nautical traffic in and around Gardner's Basin, from small boats to fishing vessels to multimillion-dollar yachts. For tourists, Gardner's Basin is the debarkation point for various boating excursions in and around Atlantic City. The tours vary from sightseeing to fishing expeditions to charters in and around the Atlantic City area. Some of these companies have walk-up opportunities, while others require a special reservation.

If you are just interested in a general tour of Atlantic City,

Cruisn 1 (609-347-7600) is your main choice. They offer cruise options that sail at various hours of the day in the summertime, including a Harbor Tour. Wintertime cruises are available by charter.

If you want to do some fishing, you may be able to do it from the shorelines of the Gardner's Basin area, or you could check out one of the three fishing cruises. **Shore Bet Fishing** (609-345-4077) offers half-day trips as well as nighttime fishing. Or you can book a seat on the **High Roller** (609-348-3474), a large pontoon boat. Though some of these companies may be available for private charters, **Atlantus Charters** (609-408-3564) makes that a priority - you can even book scuba diving or other special requests with them.

EXTREME WINDSURFING

7079 Black Horse Pike
West Atlantic City, NJ
(609) 641-4445

Getting there: Take Black Horse Pike out of Atlantic City, located next to the Hampton Inn on Lakes Bay.

Lakes Bay, located on the southern tip of Atlantic City and accessible via Black Horse Pike, is a favorite local place for water sports. As the lake is part of the larger marsh that comprises much of the Jersey Shore's coastal wetlands, it is shallow and motor-powered boats have limited access – though are seldom seen. This combined with almost consistent wind, is an ideal place for windsurfing or kite surfing.

Extreme Windsurfing, located right next to Lakes Bay and the Hampton Inn, is well-equipped for both beginning and advanced windsurfers. In addition to sales and rentals of all types of equipment and accessories, it also offers lessons on the sport. If you are interested in purchasing equipment, Extreme Windsurfing allows you to try out the latest equipment before you decide to make a purchase. Windsurfers and kite surfers should be in good physical shape, and have a basic knowledge of the sport. Lessons are available, and you must sign a comprehensive waiver before taking to the bay. The facilities on-site include the Hampton Inn, a small beach, storage, snack bar, and other amenities.

Marine Mammal Stranding Center

3625 Brigantine Blvd. (P.O. Box 773)
Brigantine, NJ
(609) 266-0537

Getting there: Take the Atlantic City Connector to the Marina District. Follow the signs to Brigantine. Center is 2 miles beyond bridge.

In 1978, the Marine Mammal Stranding Center was established to help distressed and stranded marine life in the area. Sea turtles, dolphins, whales, and other sea mammals have been assisted here, sometimes as many as 175 per year. Since opening, the center has rescued over 2,500 animals of various kinds. Originally headquartered in Gardner's Basin, the center is the only such facility in New Jersey, and has a federal and state permit to assist stranded mammals.

Visitors are allowed limited access to tour the facilities for a small donation. The actual rehabilitation center is off-limits, but visitors can still see much of the facility, including a small museum/gallery (the "Sea Life Educational Center"). There is also an on-site gift shop featuring logo shirts, CDs, and videos. Summertime hours are generally steady, but it is strongly recommended that you call ahead, as access to the facility tends to vary greatly year-round, but especially in the winter. The center operates on volunteer services and donations. On occasion, aquatic excursions may be offered (call well in advance).

SHOPPING

The recent major overhaul of Atlantic City entertainment centers includes the addition of several new shopping centers. Area resorts are shifting their gears towards more non-gambling establishments, and malls so far seem to be the general direction of this trend.

The malls and shopping areas listed here are in and around the Atlantic City area. Some will require a short drive, while others may be easily accessible from certain points on the boardwalk. However, all of them have a wide selection of shops. Shopaholics will probably find themselves at home in any one of these establishments (note that resorts may have their own shopping facilities, descriptions of which are located elsewhere in this book.)

ATLANTIC CITY OUTLETS

1801 Baltic Ave
Atlantic City, NJ
(609) 343-0081

Getting there: Just off the boardwalk, near the Bally's complex. Between Pacific and Baltic Avenues, crossed by Michigan Avenue.

Like shopping but hate the high price tag on your favorite name-brand items? Let's do some outlet shopping!

In recent years, Atlantic City has been trying to attract a crowd that is not expressly gamblers. A good way to do this is to create an outlet mall. Those who love to shop will really appreciate this new outdoor mall, located off the boardwalk, directly across from Caesars Atlantic City and Bally's Park Place.

The Walk is entirely outdoors – so you'll need to have your raincoat/sweater/whatever if you want to spend any time there in inclement weather. All the standards are represented: **Gap**, **J. Crew**, **Banana Republic**, **Mikasa**, **Guess**, and many more are on the way. As of this writing, The Walk is brand new. Many of the stores have either just opened or are opening soon. Who knows what stores the future will bring, though for the merchants it looks bright! It also contains lots of clean public spaces, restaurants such as **Subway Sandwiches** and **Starbucks**, and everything you would expect from any other quality outlet mall. The Walk is not in an enclosed area; it is a series of buildings compacted into a small section of town.

Additionally, walking along the street from shop to shop gives visitors an abbreviated history of Miss America. How? Each section is dedicated to a certain decade in Miss America's history. Engraved in the sidewalk, and on nearby signs, are biographies, pictures, and other information about past Miss America winners (if you enjoy Miss America, you may want to check out the nearby Sheraton Hotel's Miss America showcase near the hotel lobby, which features dresses, crowns, and more).

This is a great outlet mall; rivaling other top-notch shopping centers across the country, and a worthy addition to Atlantic City.

SIGANOS PLAZA

1700 Boardwalk
Atlantic City, NJ
(609) 646-2292

Getting there: Siganos Plaza is mid-boardwalk, across from The Sands casino.

A unique mix of shops and restaurants, Siganos Plaza is a small strip mall located on the boardwalk. The bright architecture of the plaza is immediately recognizable, and the colorful shops are just as eclectic on the inside as they are on the outside.

On the southern edge of the mall (next to the pedestrian walkway into The Sands/Claridge) is the unique Mediterranean restaurant **Opa**. The mall also has **Original Philly Steak**, **China One**, and **Lo Presti Pizza** for quicker bites to eat. If you have a sweet tooth, **Kandyland** has a nice assortment of tantalizing sweets. Also, **Double Rainbow Ice Cream and Coffee Café** sells just what the name suggests.

Cartoon collectibles are abundant at **Toon In**. For the sports nut, **Sports Collection** has all sorts of licensed team memorabilia and apparel (hats and jerseys). **Wacky Bear** is a unique idea – children (and adults alike) are permitted to create their own stuffed animals by stuffing and dressing a selection of adorable animals. **Spotlight** offers women's clothing, from casual wear to sleepwear to some cosmetic jewelry and accessories. **Tiki Liki** also sells clothes and different kinds of beach apparel and accessories. **Lady of Leisure** sells all sorts of women's accessories such as handbags, jewelry, and more.

Natural Health Centers offers a unique and strangely popular aqua massage; somebody lies down under a thick wall of rubber while water spray nozzles massage you up and down. If you like magnets, then you'll love **Magnetism**, a store devoted entirely to covering up your refrigerator with decorative items. Finally, for your basic magazine and candy needs, Siganos Plaza is topped off with a **Newsstand**.

DOWNTOWN ATLANTIC CITY

Northern Atlantic Avenue
Atlantic City, NJ

Atlantic Avenue is the main non-resort shopping district of Atlantic City. In particular, the strip between Trump Taj Mahal and the Atlantic City Expressway is home to many local shops. Grocery stores, mini malls, pawnshops, gold/jewelry dealers, and a few restaurants are packed into this small area, which don't seem to be related to the nearby resorts.

This is part of the "real" Atlantic City.

As these are all independent stores, there is no single opening or closing time, though many seem to close before dark. These shops are all located within a short walk to one of several resorts, but its best to explore this area during the day, when a lot of people are present (and before the Atlantic City "nightlife" crowd takes over).

FRALINGER'S SALT WATER TAFFY

Getting there: two locations on the boardwalk in Atlantic City: At Tennessee Avenue and at Bally's Park Place.

Mr. Bradley had no name for his unique taffy treats (a chewy mix of corn syrup and sugar), so he let his boardwalk patrons call it whatever they wished. On one particular day in August 1883 (the story goes), he was selling his taffy as usual. But a nasty storm blew salt water all over poor Mr. Bradley's stand. After the storm passed, a young girl ordered from Mr. Bradley some of his taffy, which had been drenched in the ocean's salt water. "Don't you mean 'Salt Water Taffy'?" Mr. Bradley asked the girl. Mr. Fralinger – interested in opening a taffy stand of his own - was standing nearby and overheard the remark, and the name "Salt Water Taffy" was born.

Those who have enjoyed Salt Water Taffy in candy stores across the country may not know that this treat – hardly salty or watery – is an Atlantic City original. Fralinger's Salt Water Taffy popularized the treat after he opened up his own shop in 1885. Today the shops are full-fledged candy stores, but the taffy selection is extensive. Choose from many, many different flavors, mix and match your candy pieces, or buy a box with a pre-sorted mix.

Fralinger's has two locations on the Atlantic City Boardwalk today. There are also locations in nearby Ocean City and Cape May. Those afar may also order taffy online at www.fralingers.com or by calling 1-800-93-TAFFY. Though many companies may produce Salt Water Taffy today, Fralinger's is "officially" the original.

SHORE MALL

6725 Black Horse Pike
Egg Harbor Township, NJ
(609) 484-9500

Getting there: Take Black Horse Pike / Albany Ave / U.S. Route 40 all the way out of Atlantic City.

The Shore Mall is about 10 miles out of Atlantic City, and features many of the shopping plaza essentials. The main stores include **Circuit City, Value City,** and **Burlington Coat Factory.** This one-story has outdoor access to many stores directly from the parking lot.

Other stores on the premises include **Boscov's, Radio Shack, Foot Locker, Angel Nails, Kay Bee Toys, Game Gallery, Beachcomber Collectibles, Atlantic Books, GNC,** and many more; there are about 60 stores in total. In addition, the 14-screen **Frank's Family Cinema** is nearby; one of the closest multiplex movie theaters to the Atlantic City Boardwalk. There is also an **Action Zone Arcade** and **Wired – Interactive Computer Video Games,** for the electronically inclined.

HISTORIC SMITHVILLE

1 New York Road
Smithville, NJ
(609) 652-7777

Getting there: Take U.S. Route 30 / White Horse Pike out of Atlantic City, and turn north onto U.S. Route 9 for about 10 miles.

In 1787 there was only Smithville Inn. Built on a common stagecoach route and run by James Baremore, the Inn eventually became a popular resting place for weary travelers, as not many houses or other establishments existed in the area. But, as the years went by and more area commerce arose, the need for an Inn at this spot diminished, until the property finally was abandoned at around the turn of the 20th century. In the early 1950s Fred and Ethel Noyes purchased the structure and restored it into a restaurant, and the seven acres surrounding the Inn would eventually become known as The Towne of Historic Smithville.

Today, the seven-acre "town", a National Historic Landmark, is a re-creation of what an east coast village looked like in the 1700s. Cobblestone streets align village buildings, a Village Green, complete with gazebo, a small lake, and nearly every building is packed with handcrafts and thingamajigs for sale. Many of the buildings, purchased by the Noyes, were from sites all over this part of New Jersey. Historic Smithville is a must-see for anybody and can be a particularly fun afternoon for families with children.

The collection of shops is eclectic and shopping here can be very relaxing and enjoyable. Stores include **The Candle Shoppe, The Christmas Shoppe, Cozy Fireside Treasures, The Jewelry Box, Pocket Full of Posies, Country Folk**, and dozens more, including places to eat, from a quick bite to a lavish multi-course dinner. Aside from shopping, visitors may enjoy paddle boating on the lake, a mini train ride; a remote-controlled boat course, a carousel, and an old-time arcade. Although Historic Smithville is open year-round, some of the other attractions are only available during the warmer months. **The Smithville Inn**, of course, is still there. It serves as a meeting and banquet facility. Weddings here are common, but they also serve lunch, dinner, and occasionally brunch.

Historic Smithville also has a small hospitable lodging facility available. **The Colonial Inn** (615 East Moss Mill Road, Smithville, NJ, 609-748-8999, http://www.colonialinnsmithville.com) is a bed and breakfast-style located directly on the grounds. It is open year-round and features eight rooms, some of which overlook the lake. The rooms are decorated to reflect the period. Rates include private bathrooms and standard hotel amenities. However, though Historic Smithville is very family-friendly, small children are not encouraged not to stay at The Colonial Inn.

Throughout the year, Historic Smithville redecorates itself with holiday themes. Throughout August and September, it is host to special events, such as concerts and sidewalk sales. One of the largest events is Oktoberfest, where arts and crafts abound. During this time, there is also a "Haunted Train Ride" on weekends. For the holidays, there is a "Christmas Train Ride" and Santa Claus himself may even make a personal appearance.

Historic Smithville has enough to see and do to occupy an entire day, particularly during the summertime. Its small size and themed nature are second only to its impeccable charm. Near a city with big lights and flashy facades, the quaint and beautiful Smithville is an absolute breath of fresh air, and a must-see.

HAMILTON MALL

4403 Black Horse Pike
Mays Landing, NJ
(609) 646-8326

Getting there: Take Black Horse Pike (Albany Ave / US Route 40) out of Atlantic City for several miles until you reach the mall.

A few short miles from the shore on Black Horse Pike is the large Hamilton Mall. As it is a more "regular" mall in the Atlantic City area (in that its not located on a Pier or part of a resort), it compensates by having a wide selection of shops, both large and small.

The list of shops is way too extensive to name here, but they have **Macy's, Sears, Gymboree, Limited Too, The Children's Place, JCPenny, Express, Gap, Wilson Leather, Pac Sun, Victoria's Secret, Wet Seal, Foot Locker, Electronics Boutique, Radio Shack, Sam Goody, Suncoast Motion Picture Company**, several cell phone stores, **Claire's Boutique, Zales, GNC, K-B Toys**, and many, many others. There are over 140 stores and restaurants in Hamilton Mall. For a complete list of stores and phone numbers, you can visit their website at http://www.hamiltonmall.com.

CLUBS AND NIGHTLIFE

Atlantic City is an up-all-night kind of place. The casinos are open 24-hours a day, 7 days a week, which naturally gives rise to other possibilities of nightlife. Like Las Vegas, Atlantic City is famous for its after-hours entertainment opportunities. While some major resort hotels offer generally safe, upscale clubbing experiences (particularly **Casbah** at Trump Taj Mahal, **Mixx** at the Borgata, and **The Wave** at Trump Marina), the city itself has numerous other ways to kill time before the sun rises. Some of these ways are more scandalous than others, so for those wishing for a good time past sunset, be sure to keep your wits about you.

Atlantic City's nightlife is strictly for adults! Even the resorts' clubs and bars are meant for those over 21 (sometimes over 18), and the clientele, many times broke, intoxicated and tipsily walking from the nearest casino, are in no mental state to behave themselves. Be warned that children should not venture from the resorts during the nighttime hours. Though the boardwalk and resort areas are predominantly safe, children should not be left alone to wander. While this is true in all places, it holds particularly true for Atlantic City. Because of the vast dichotomy between resortland and cityland, mere steps away from the casino's entrance could bring any unsuspecting wanderer into an area that he or she would prefer not enter. Atlantic City streets off the resort properties are incredibly diverse. You may find yourself one moment under the glitzy umbrella of a resort, and in the next moment on a deserted city street. Keep your wits about you.

That being said, if you're up to experiencing Atlantic City's nightlife, this section describes some of the wide range of entertainment and activities available, besides gambling, during the nighttime hours. Atlantic City nights begin at approximately 8-9PM, and facilities will close between about 2-3AM (except for casinos, of course).

CASINOS

Every casino in Atlantic City, whether it is on the boardwalk or in the Marina District, is open 24 hour a day, 7 days a week. Casino gambling is by far the #1 nighttime entertainment option in Atlantic City, and very likely on the entire Jersey Shore. Few other venues across the country have such a wide operating schedule, and will be crowded even in the wee hours of the morning.

A gaming day in Atlantic City starts at 6:00AM and runs until 5:59AM the following morning. No matter what time of year you intend on visiting Atlantic City, and no matter which resort you visit, and what time of day you go, there will always, *always* be activity on the casino floor.

But which casino is right for you? That is entirely your choice. Many people gamble only in the resort in which they are staying, whereas others casino-hop across the boardwalk. Many people are devoted to one single players' club, whereas others have thick wallets with club cards from each of the resorts. One of the best features of Atlantic City, of course, is the freedom to move around with ease.

CLUB TRU

9 South Martin Luther King Jr. Blvd
Atlantic City, NJ
(609) 347-3500

Getting there: Between Artic Avenue and Atlantic Avenue, on Martin Luther King Jr. Boulevard. Close to Bally's Claridge Tower.

For locals as well as tourists, Club Tru is Atlantic City's mecca of nighttime entertainment. It has the organization of a resort – visitors who enter can choose between different attractions located directly on the property. The club requires an admission charge, which allows access to the various facilities within. The charge varies from day to day and depending on your situation (ladies, for example, sometimes get free admission before midnight).

The indoor complex is huge – three floors full of various nightlife attractions. The main attractions are the dance halls, **Club Tru** and **Studio Six**. Here, the lights flash and the sweaty pulse of DJ-spinned music rocks the house all through the night. The **Tru Energy Bar** has caffeine-infused alcoholic beverages to keep your heart rate up. For a more relaxed visitor, **Joe's Sports Bar** on the ground floor is a place to have a beer and relax, while still being close to the action. For a more upscale drink surrounding, the **Perfect 10 Martini Lounge** and **4c's VIP Lounge** cater to the more expensive drinks and more relaxing surroundings. But remember – it is still a club, so just about anywhere you decide to drink is going to have a nighttime pulse.

Club Tru packs its calendar throughout the year with various themed nights – particularly during the slower weekday times. But on Friday and Saturday night, expect a long line to enter the club and various promotions and "shows" to keep you there. They frequently give out cash prizes for competitions such as "sexiest female" and "sexiest male" of the night.

Club Tru is also directly connected – through an inside corridor – to the **Surfside Resort Hotel** (18 South Mt. Vernon Avenue 609-347-7873). This is a smaller hotel with 50 rooms, ranging from standard size to a penthouse suite, each with an individual style. The reasonable room rates and close proximity to the boardwalk and Club Tru makes this a good spot if you plan on experiencing a lot of Atlantic City's nightlife. The hotel stands well on its own, with on-property establishments such as an outdoor pool and sun deck and various drinking establishments.

STRIP CLUBS

In all fairness, there are strip clubs in some form in nearly every city across the country. But for Atlantic City, like Las Vegas, adult clubs like this bear special significance. As a city profiting on another escapade – gambling – strip clubs seem to be a natural extension of the activities already commonplace. This is both a blessing and a curse; depending on your whims. Atlantic City is naturally beautiful as a seaside resort, and can potentially be fruitful with many other, more family-friendly activities. This is different than Las Vegas, where nothing but desert surrounds the oasis, so diversions must be created. Nonetheless, these strip clubs play a role in Atlantic City's current situation, and any traveler (or travel guide) choosing to ignore this side of America's first seaside resort will simply not be able to paint a full picture.

Atlantic City has several strip clubs either around the boardwalk or easily accessible by car. Strip clubs in this city tend to be popular places for locals as well as travelers visiting the casinos. Don't expect the New York City or Las Vegas showiness of these clubs. These are generally small, smoky, and congested places filled mostly with men and a few scantily clad women. Cover charges are almost unavoidable. Generally the sport in these facilities is male bonding coupled with girl watching. Depending on the establishment, you may be able to buy alcoholic drinks, backrubs, or "other entertainment" from the dancers.

The only all-nude strip club in Atlantic City is **Bare Exposure** (2203 Pacific Avenue, 609-449-0999). Located just south of the Trump Plaza self-park lot, Bare Exposure is also completely alcohol-free. However, patrons are allowed to bring alcoholic drinks in from the outside (such as beers from a nearby convenience store). The room is small and smoky, and generally very crowded, especially during weekend night hours. Three small stages feature dancers, and a back room allows for private dances. Local reviews of Bare Exposure give this establishment a high rating.

Located about two blocks south on Pacific Avenue is **Playground** (2405 Pacific Avenue, 609-347-1234). Within walking distance to Trump Plaza and very close to Bare Exposure, Playground is not an all-nude club, though they do have inexpensive drinks. It is also a smaller and quieter place.

Also near the boardwalk, further south, is **Coconutz** (30 South Florida Avenue, 609-449-0033). Coconutz touts itself as more of a bikini bar, since there is less nudity here than at other strip clubs. It has a full bar and especially caters to bachelor parties. The crowd is mostly local, as it is located further from a major resort than other strip clubs.

Delilah's Den (201 East Delilah Road, Pleasantville, 609-383-0666) is a short drive away from the boardwalk. Located in nearby Pleasantville, Delilah's is one of the most well-advertised and popular strip clubs in the Atlantic City area. This is a non-nude club, very similar to the ones located near the boardwalk, but a recent renovation has brought a little more flare to an otherwise standard place.

There are many more strip clubs in and around the Atlantic City area than are listed here. Local newspapers such as *The Atlantic City Weekly* (available free at most information kiosks) on occasion have advertisements in their classified information section.

OTHER NIGHTLIFE

Again, heed this warning: *venture from the resorts or boardwalk at night, and you may not like where the road takes you!* There is an abundance of escort services in Atlantic City. Some of these are legitimate, but many are covers for prostitution. I state again, so take this to mean what you will: there *is* prostitution in Atlantic City. On certain roads, at certain times, these services are *abundant*, particularly in the summer. Prostitutes generally do not seek business on the boardwalk or in the resorts (though it does happen). Instead, they haunt the nearest roads to the boardwalk resorts – more specifically, Pacific and Atlantic Avenues. (I am pointing this out simply as information and to help you, the traveler, possibly avoid being surprised.)

But there are alternatives. The beach and boardwalk are open all night, and particularly around the brightly lit casinos during the summertime, these areas see trickles of people even in the wee hours of the morning. The casinos open directly to the boardwalk, so it can offer a nice breath of nighttime fresh air for gamblers. The beach, however, is not patrolled and has no lifeguards at anytime, so a night stroll down the beach may provide some quiet relaxation time (but be careful – the ocean is dangerous). Night swimming is not recommended.

Finally, since the Atlantic Ocean is east, the sunrises in Atlantic City are unbeatable. Lying on the beach or sitting on the boardwalk during sun-up is a romantic way to either start or end your day (depending on how late you go to sleep).

RESOURCES

This section contains ways you can begin to plan your first or next Atlantic City vacation, as well as a listing of select restaurants, accommodations, and additional Internet and print resources.

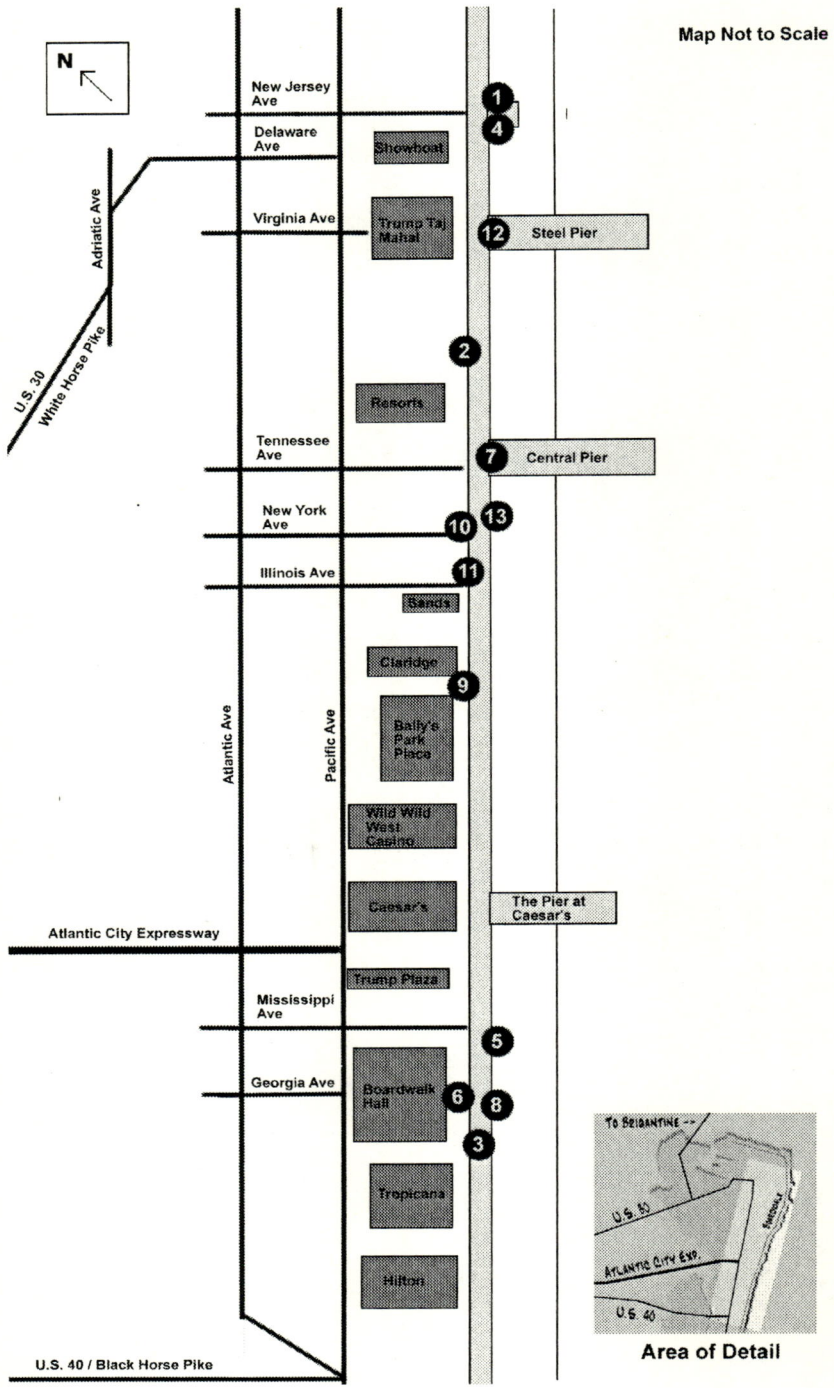

BOARDWALK ATTRACTIONS

Following is a list of select attractions, other than the resorts, that are located directly on the boardwalk. Descriptions for these attractions can be found elsewhere in this book.

(1)   Atlantic City Art Center   (609) 347-5839
       New Jersey Avenue

(2)   Atlantic City Boardwalk Arcade   (609) 345-3710
       Ocean Avenue

(3)   Playcade Arcade   (609) 345-8260
       2629 Boardwalk

(4)   Atlantic City Historical Museum   (609) 347-5839
       New Jersey Avenue

(5)   Atlantic City Miniature Golf   (609) 347-1661
       Mississippi Avenue

(6)   Boardwalk Hall   (609) 348-7000
       2301 Boardwalk

(7)   Central Pier Arcade & Speedway   (609) 345-5219
       Tennessee Avenue

(8)   Kennedy Plaza   N/A
       Georgia Avenue

(9)   New Jersey Korean War Memorial   N/A
       Brighton Park

(10)   Ripley's *Believe It or Not!* Museum   (609) 347-2001
       New York Avenue

(11)   Sigano's Plaza   (609) 641-4931
       1717 Boardwalk

(12)   Steel Pier   (866) 386-6659
       Virginia Avenue

(13)   WOW VR Live!   (609) 347-1661
       New York Avenue

RESORT SUMMARY

Resort	Address	Contact	Resort Size	Eateries***	Shops***	Pool	Beach	Notables	Page
Atlantic City Hilton	Boston & Boardwalk	(609) 347-7111	Small	10	2	Indoor	Yes	Larger-than-usual rooms	51
Bally's Atlantic City*	Park Place & Boardwalk	(609) 340-2000	Large	23	8	Indoor	Yes**	Three Casinos in One	75
Borgata	1 Borgata Way	(609) 317-1000	Large	11	8	Indoor	No	Newest Resort in AC	117
Caesars Atlantic City	2100 Pacific Ave	(609) 348-4411	Medium	17	8	Outdoor	Yes	Future Site of "The Pier"	67
Harrah's Atlantic City	777 Harrah's Blvd.	(609) 441-5600	Medium	9	2	Indoor	No	Large Casino Chain	113
Resorts	1133 Boardwalk	(609) 344-6000	Medium	6	3	Indoor	Yes	First Casino in AC	97
Sands	Indiana & Brighton Park	(609) 441-4000	Small	7	1	No	Yes**	Smallest Resort	93
Showboat	801 Boardwalk	(609) 343-4000	Medium	8	1	No	Yes	French Quarter Buffet	107
Tropicana	Brighton & Boardwalk	(609) 340-4000	Large	21	34	In/Outdoor	Yes	The Quarter	55
Trump Marina	Huron & Brigantine Blvd	(609) 441-2000	Small	8	12	Outdoor	No	Farley State Marina on-site	123
Trump Plaza	Mississippi & Boardwalk	(609) 441-6000	Small	8	3	Indoor	Yes	First Trump Casino	61
Trump Taj Mahal	1000 Boardwalk	(609) 449-1000	Medium	12	14	Indoor	Yes	Near Steel Pier	101

Resort Size: Small = less than 1,000 guest rooms, Medium = 1,000 - 1,500 guest rooms, large = More than 1,500 guest rooms

* Bally's Atlantic City includes Bally's Park Place, Claridge Tower, and Bally's Wild Wild West Casino.
** Sands & Claridge (Bally's) are 1 block from the boardwalk.
*** Approximately

Please note that there is no guarantee as to the accuracy of the information on this page.

MUST-SEE ATTRACTIONS

In addition to the resorts, Atlantic City has a collection of excellent area attractions. Following is what I think are the best ones, and worth a visit.

Attraction	When to Visit	In/Outdoors	Notables	Page
Absecon Lighthouse	Any time	Indoors	Great view of Atlantic City from the top	152
Atlantic City Outlets	Any time	Outdoor mall, shops inside	Discount shopping on brand name merchandise	169
Batsto Village	Any time but winter	Outdoors	Historic town	162
Boardwalk Hall	During an event	Indoors	Huge indoor convention center	139
Edwin B. Forsythe N.W.F.	Weather permitting	Outdoors, but stay in car	Natural Jersey Shore, drive-thru reserve	161
Historic Smithville	Any time	Outdoor mall, shops inside	Arts and crafts shop and small rides	173
Lucy the Elephant	Any time but winter	Indoors	Unusual museum of Jersey Shore history	153
Noyes Museum	Any time	Indoors	Art museum	159
Ocean Life Center	Any time	Indoors	Jersey Shore-themed aquarium	156
Renault Winery	Spring or summer	Both	Vineyard, upscale restaurant, and golf course	157
Ripley's *Believe it or Not!*	Any time	Indoors	Young seekers of world oddities	150
Steel Pier	Summertime	Outdoors	Midway-type rides and games	131
Storybook Land	Any time, limited off-season hrs.	Outdoors	Small amusement park for very young children	137

Select Theme Restaurants and Chains

Name	Location(s)	Features
Auntie Anne's	Trump Taj Mahal, Trump Marina	Pretzels
Burger King	2700 Boardwalk (near Tropicana)	fast food
Corky's Ribs & BBQ	Tropicana	Memphis-based rib franchise
Hard Rock Café	Trump Taj Mahal	Music Memorabilia
Hooters	Tropicana and Trump Marina	Burgers, fried foods, and busty wait staff
Johnny Rockets	Bally's Park Place	Old-fashioned diner-style
McDonald's	Right off the AC Expressway	fast food
Planet Hollywood	Caesars Atlantic City	Movie Memorabilia
Rainforest Café	Trump Plaza	Dine in a rainforest
Starbucks	7 locations in Atlantic City	Coffee
Subway Sandwiches	Atlantic City Outlets: "The Walk"	Sandwiches & Salads

Please note that there is no guarantee as to the accuracy of the information on this page.

The listing here is by no means all-inclusive. It is merely a sampling of the restaurants.

SELECT ACCOMMODATIONS

> *Note:* this section contains only a selection of the hotel and motel options in Atlantic City, with various qualities, rates, and amenities. It gives the overall perspective of accommodations available.

Besides the major casino resorts in Atlantic City, there are literally dozens of hotels and motels that pepper the Atlantic City area. Many of these are popular hotel chains, while a few are independently operated. Black Horse Pike and White Horse Pike, the two main roads other than the Atlantic City Expressway that connect Atlantic City to the mainland (from the south and from the north, respectively) are also home to many of the areas smaller hotels. Since the marshy area surrounding Absecon Island is largely uninhabitable, the hotels located on one of these two roads may require a drive of several miles to reach the boardwalk, since you must first traverse the marshes. Nonetheless, they provide a good selection of accommodations that are generally much cheaper than the casinos. Some have restaurants or a limited other amenities on-property.

If you are determined to stay as close to the boardwalk as possible, there are also many non-resort hotels in the main Atlantic City area, though the closer you get to the boardwalk, the more expensive the accommodations (but the less driving you will have to do to reach the beach).

The non-resort hotels in Atlantic City vary tremendously in terms of quality and type of accommodation. Larger hotels (more than 100 rooms) tend to – but do not always – have an interior corridor, whereas the rest are motel-style. Some resorts have on-property restaurants or fitness centers, while other do not. Some have indoor or outdoor pools, whereas others do not.

NOTE: The information listed here does not qualify any of these hotels, but instead provides critical information so that you will be able investigate them more thoroughly yourself. It is strongly recommended that you seek information from other sources before you decide to stay in one of the following hotels or motels. The hotel information provided here has been checked for accuracy but the information here is not guaranteed to be correct. Since hotels tend to go in and out of business, be sure to call and inquire first.

BOARDWALK AREA

These hotels and motels are located near the boardwalk (and, in some instances, directly on the boardwalk). Generally, by staying in these hotels, you will be able to access the beach and resorts after only a short walk. As the resort section is about a 2-mile stretch on a single path, most of these hotels are on one of the two main roads immediately parallel to the boardwalk. On the other hand, attractions not located on the boardwalk may require a car anyway, so it may not matter how close you stay, depending on your vacation plans.

DOWNBEACH HOTELS

These hotels are located in the Downbeach section of Atlantic City, which is home to the Tropicana and Hilton resorts, as well as Boardwalk Hall. The hotels in this section are generally small motels, with varying qualities. A few have pools and other amenities.

Rodeway Inn Atlantic City
3601 Pacific Avenue
22 Rooms
(609) 348-9111
Features: southerly location with short walking distance to boardwalk.

Holiday Inn Boardwalk
115 Chelsea Ave & Boardwalk
220 Rooms
(609) 348-2200
Features: On boardwalk, next to Tropicana, food, pool, fitness

El Greco Motel
3200 Pacific Avenue
58 Rooms
(609) 345-6195
Features: short walking distance to the boardwalk

Howard Johnson Hotel Atlantic City
Chelsea Avenue & Boardwalk
121 Rooms
(609) 344-7071
Features: on the boardwalk, near Tropicana, pool & fitness.

Days Inn Atlantic City
112 S Morris Ave & Boardwalk
105 Rooms
(609) 344-6101
Features: on boardwalk, dining on property.

Econo Lodge Beach Block
3001 Pacific Avenue
65 Rooms
(609) 344-2925
Features: short walking distance to the boardwalk.

MIDTOWN AND UPTOWN HOTELS

As the Atlantic City Expressway heads directly into the midtown resort area, the off-resort hotels in this section sometimes feature additional amenities and a more resort-like ambience.

Sheraton Atlantic City Convention Center Hotel
2 Miss America Way
504 Rooms
(609) 344-3535
Features: Near Convention Cntr.

Comfort Inn Atlantic City
154 South Kentucky Avenue
80 Rooms
(609) 348-4000
Features: 2 blocks from boardwalk, Near Bally's.

Econo Lodge Boardwalk
117 South Kentucky Avenue
51 Rooms
(609) 344-9093
Features: Near Bally's complex.
Pool on-property.

Super 8 Atlantic City
175-181 South Tennessee Avenue
68 Rooms
(609) 344-8956
Features: short walk to the boardwalk

Quality Inn Beach Block
113 South Carolina Avenue
203 Rooms
(609) 345-7070
Features: close to the boardwalk, meeting rooms on-property.

Best Western Envoy Inn
1416 Pacific Avenue
76 Rooms
(609) 344-7116
Features: Long walk or short drive to the boardwalk. Closest to Sands and Resorts.

Howard Johnson Downtown
Tennessee and Pacific Ave.
71 Rooms
(609) 344-4193
Features: Restaurant, outdoor pool, close to the boardwalk.

Rodeway Inn
124 S. North Carolina Avenue
25 Rooms
(609) 345-0155
Features: Close to the boardwalk, Trump Taj Mahal & Resorts.

WHITE HORSE PIKE AREA

When entering Atlantic City from the north, the only option is Absecon Avenue, White Horse Pike, U.S. Route 30. While providing a spectacular view of the Atlantic City skyline across a large marshy plain, the road and surrounding area provides a selection of hotel and motel accommodations. The establishments listed here are not on Absecon Island (or within Atlantic City), but may provide some good values and a location that encourages exploration of the surrounding area. Hotels in this section are at least five miles from the boardwalk.

Heading south on the Garden State Parkway, access the White Horse Pike hotel area by using exit 40. The Marina District is easy to access from this exit, and the signs on the Parkway allude to this.

Comfort Inn North
539 Absecon Boulevard
Absecon, NJ
205 Rooms
(609) 641-7272
Features: Fitness room, Atlantic City skyline view.

Travelodge Atlantic City Absecon
316 East Absecon Boulevard
Absecon, NJ
27 Rooms
(609) 652-0904
Features: Outdoor swimming pool

Fairfield Inn Absecon
405 East Absecon Boulevard
Absecon, NJ
200 Rooms
(609) 646-5000
Features: pool on-property, restaurants nearby

Dr. Jonathon Pitney House
57 N. Shore Road
Absecon, NJ
10 Rooms
(888) 774-8639
Features: Historical significance (see elsewhere in this book)

Days Inn Absecon NJ 450 Club
224 E White Horse Pike
Absecon, NJ
102 Rooms
(609) 652-2200
Features: on-property restaurant, outdoor pool

Quality Inn and Suites
202 East White Horse Pike
Galloway, NJ
50 Rooms
(609) 652-3020
Features: Pool, fitness room

Econo Lodge Absecon
328 White Horse Pike
Absecon, NJ
62 Rooms
(609) 652-3300
Features: Near some restaurants.

Rodeway Inn Absecon
547 Absecon Boulevard
Absecon, NJ
30 Rooms
(609) 646-3867
Features: Near some restaurants

Holiday Inn Express Absecon
655 White Horse Pike
Absecon, NJ
49 Rooms
(609) 383-9070
Features: Fitness and meeting rooms, newer hotel

Best Western Garden State Inn
701 White Horse Pike
Absecon, NJ
62 Rooms
(609) 645-0697
Features: Pool on property, restaurants nearby.

Hampton Inn Atlantic City Absecon
240 East White Horse Pike
Absecon, NJ
129 Rooms
(609) 652-2500
Features: meeting rooms, pool access, nearby restaurants

Howard Johnson Express Inn Absecon
248 East Absecon Blvd.
Absecon, NJ
42 Rooms
(609) 748-2300
Features: Restaurants nearby.

BLACK HORSE PIKE AREA

Entering Atlantic City on the southern route takes you on Black Horse Pike, through West Atlantic City. The road ultimately takes you to the Downbeach resort area, with closer access to attractions south of Atlantic City (such as Lucy the Elephant, and the cities of Margate, Ventnor, and Longport). The hotels along this road are much closer to the boardwalk than those on White Horse Pike (starting at about two miles). Some hotels may have a shuttle service; call them for details. As with all other vehicular arteries, before entering Atlantic City, Black Horse Pike crosses a marshy area. Some of the hotels here are located on marshy Lakes Bay.

Quality Inn Casino City
500 N. Albany Ave.
85 Rooms
(609) 344-9085
Features: Near Stadium

Clarion Hotel Bayside Resort
8029 Black Horse Pike
110 Rooms
(609) 641-4329
Features: outdoor pool, fitness

Ramada Limited
8037 Black Horse Pike
West Atlantic City, NJ
141 Rooms
(609) 646-5220
Features: outdoor pool

Hampton Inn AC Bayside
7079 Black Horse Pike
West Atlantic City, NJ
143 Rooms
(609) 484-1900
Features: on Lakes Bay

Comfort Inn West
7095 Black Horse Pike
West Atlantic City, NJ
189 Rooms
(609) 645-1818
Features: outdoor pool, meeting rooms

Best Western Atlantic City West Extended Stay & Suites
701 Black Horse Pike
Pleasantville, NJ
68 Rooms
(609) 646-5515
Features: newer hotel, mini-suites, indoor pool and fitness center

Quality Inn Pleasantville
1012 Black Horse Pike
Pleasantville, NJ
44 Rooms
(609) 641-4200
Features: pool, meeting rooms

Clarion Hotel Convention Center Atlantic City
6821 Black Horse Pike
Egg Harbor Township, NJ
213 Rooms
(609) 272-0200
Features: casino shuttle, pool, restaurant

Comfort Inn Victorian
6817 Black Horse Pike
Pleasantville, NJ
117 Rooms
(609) 646 - 8880
Features: outdoor pool, fitness center, meeting rooms

Holiday Inn Express Atlantic City
6811 Black Horse Pike
West Atlantic City, NJ
197 Rooms
(609) 484-1500
Features: new renovation, pool, fitness center, restaurant

Camping

The New Jersey Pine Barrens is just minutes away from Atlantic City. It provides an abundance of outdoor activities, not the least of which is both public and private campgrounds. If camping is your thing, then you won't be hard-pressed to find a campground to your liking less than 30 miles away.

For rustic camping, the public campgrounds available in the nearby Wharton State Forest – New Jersey's largest forest preserve, offer several campsites accessible either by hiking or by car, or both. Permits are required to utilize these sites, and there are minimal amenities, if any (See the *Wharton State Forest* section for more information.)

If you want to camp but want to be surrounded by some modern conveniences (such as showers, swimming pools, etc.) then the area's private campgrounds may be a good choice. Depending on time of year and availability, these sites may offer for rent trailers, cabins, as well as campsites with or without electrical/water hookups. Call in advance to make reservations and ensure that the amenities you desire will be available.

Yogi Bear's Jellystone Park
1079 12th Avenue
Mays Landing, NJ
163 various sites
(609) 476-2811
Features: Very family-friendly, pool & park, planned activities

Whippoorwill Campground
810 South Shore Road
Marmora, NJ
(609) 391-3458
Features: Close to Ocean City, 20 miles from Atlantic City

Evergreen Woods
106 East Moss Mill Road
Pomona, NJ
(609) 652-1577
Features: closest private campsite to Atlantic City, lakefront property

SELECT RESTAURANTS

Note: this section contains only a small selection of the vast array of dining options in Atlantic City, of various cuisines and qualities. It gives the overall perspective of restaurants available.

Aside from the plethora of restaurants located within the resorts themselves, Atlantic City boasts a wide range of dining options, from casual to fine dining and everything in between. There are small establishments and large banquet halls. From fresh seafood to Italian to Mexican to Chinese cuisine, the options for eats in Atlantic City is immense – it boasts more high-class restaurants than any other point along the Jersey Shore. Restaurants within resorts are not listed here; dining information for these locations can be found within the description of the resorts themselves.

Atlantic City restaurants tend to open and close, change names or cuisines at the drop of a hat. Following is a list of select restaurants in the area. Critical contact information is provided, as well as price, cuisine, and basic atmospheric information. It is highly recommended that you contact any of these establishments to confirm availability. However, if a restaurant is of particular importance to Atlantic City history and/or has been around for a while, it will be indicated by an asterisk (*)

after the establishment's name. The average price of an entrée is used to determine the establishment's price rating.

Prices are indicated as follows:

$$$ - Expensive (More than $20 per entrée)
$$ - Moderate ($10 - $20 per entrée)
$ - Inexpensive ($10 or less per entrée)

Angelo's Fairmount Tavern (609) 344-2439 Price: $$
2300 Fairmont Avenue
http://www.angelosfairmounttavern.com

Cuisine
Italian

Features
Casual, family dining.

Angeloni's II * (609) 344-7875 Price: $$
2400 Arctic Avenue
http://www.angelonis.com

Cuisine
Italian

Features
Casual, extensive wine selection.

Atlantic City Bar & Grill (609) 348-8080 Price: $$
1219 Pacific Avenue
http://www.acbarandgrill.com

Cuisine
Mixed

Features
Casual; fare varies from pizza to lobsters.

Babalu Grill (609) 572-9898 Price: $$
2020 Atlantic Avenue
http://www.serioussteaks.com

Cuisine
Latin/Steaks

Features
Casual bar/restaurant, near AC Outlets.

Chelsea Cafe   (609) 347-7194   Price: $
1523 Boardwalk

Cuisine   **Features**
Pizza   Take out or dine in, located on the boardwalk.

Dock's Oyster House *   (609) 345-0092   Price: $$$
2405 Atlantic Avenue
http://www.docksoysterhouse.com

Cuisine   **Features**
Seafood   Friendly fine dining, raw bar, est. 1897.

Flying Cloud Cafe   (609) 345-8222   Price: $
800 North New Hampshire Avenue
http://www.atlanticcityflyingcloud.com

Cuisine   **Features**
Seafood   Local feel, outdoor deck, live music.

Hunan Chinese Restaurant   (609) 348-5946   Price: $
2323 Atlantic Avenue

Cuisine   **Features**
Chinese   Inexpensive Chinese take-out/dine-in.

Imperial Inn   (609) 347-8810   Price: $/$$
3124 Atlantic Avenue

Cuisine   **Features**
Chinese   Casual Chinese, Szechwan, Mandarin

Irish Pub & Inn   (609) 344-9063   Price: $
164 Saint James Place
http://www.theirishpub.com

Cuisine   **Features**
Irish American   Bar/lounge, Irish drinks and snack foods.

| Knife & Fork Inn | (609) 344-1133 | Price: $$$ |

Atlantic Avenue & Pacific Avenue
http://www.knifeandforkinn.com

Cuisine
Seafood & Steak

Features
Fine dining; Renaissance theme, est. 1912.

| Los Amigos | (609) 344-2293 | Price: $$ |

1926 Atlantic Avenue
http://www.logamigosrest.com

Cuisine
Mexican

Features
Casual, Tex-Mex, unusual façade.

| Mama Mott's Restaurant | (609) 348-6378 | Price: $$$ |

151 South New York Avenue
http://www.mamamotts.com

Cuisine
Italian, Seafood

Features
Fine dining, reminiscent of Little Italy.

| Opa | (609) 344-0094 | Price: $$ |

1743 Boardwalk
http://www.opa1.com

Cuisine
Mediterranean

Features
Hip, casual/fine dining on the boardwalk

| Tun Tavern | (609) 347-7800 | Price: $$$ |

2 Ocean Way
http://www.tuntavern.com

Cuisine
Steak & Seafood

Features
Casual/fine dining, Brewery on-property.

White House Sub Shop *   (609) 345-8599   Price: $
2301 Arctic Avenue

Cuisine
Sandwiches

Features
Famous subs, landmark restaurant

Wonder Bar   (609) 345-8599   Price: $$/$$$
3701 Sunset Avenue
http://www.wonderbarac.com

Cuisine
Seafd & Sndwch

Features
Fine dining on the water, seasonal patio

Travel Scenarios

Following are vacation possibilities under various circumstances. Atlantic City vacations are tremendously flexible and hassle-free. Eat when you want, explore where you want, do what you want. These scenarios keep your options open and give you the freedom to allow your vacation to unfold however you want. Note: The total price is a very broad reference, and unless otherwise stated it includes 1 room, and 2 meals a day for each member of the party.

One-Day Getaway

Vacation Time: *1 Day*
Best Time to Go: *Any time, any day*
Total Price: *As little as $8 - $10 per person*

Atlantic City is ultra-accessible, particularly for individuals without access to a car and in a major urban area. If you fit this description, you're in luck, as your vacation can be extremely inexpensive.

Either drive or, from a major metropolitan area (such as Washington, DC, New York City, or Philadelphia), board a casino bus service to your favorite Atlantic City resort. When you arrive, spend the day roaming the resort. Check out the restaurants, the health club, the shopping, and even the beach if it is nearby and weather permitting. Stroll the boardwalk and take in the fresh ocean air. When you're ready to return, simply board the bus (or drive) from the resort and make your way back home.

Recommendations: The best resorts for strolling arbitrarily and enjoying the beach include: Tropicana, Trump Taj Mahal, and Bally's Atlantic City. Many times, however, people will want to catch a show in one of the many venues in Atlantic City. If you are interested in the entertainment, check the resort's entertainment schedules in advance, as you may not be able to buy tickets at the box office.

On the Cheap

Vacation Time: *2 Days*
Best Time to Go: *Winter weekday*
Total Price: *Less than $120 for up to 2 people*

The cheapest time to visit Atlantic City is Tuesday - Thursday in the winter, where prices for an on-boardwalk resort can plummet to around $50 if you shop around. However, if you must stay in the summer or on the weekend, consider an off-resort hotel (you may need to rent a car if you don't already own one.)

Plan your travel so that you arrive mid-afternoon, and are able to check-in to your hotel at around 4:00 PM. Once you're situated, its time to enjoy the resort. Start off by eating an early dinner at a moderately-priced restaurant. Then enjoy the evening strolling the resort and the boardwalk. If you're near The Walk, Atlantic City's outlet mall, you may be able to get some shopping in before the stores close. Also, since you have an entire night, you may wish to consider exploring other nearby resorts as well; so don't feel confined to the one in which you are staying. In the later hours, night owls may be able to enjoy one of several night clubs, either on-property or off. Enjoy a late-night drink before heading off to sleep.

If you're an early riser, spend the morning swimming, if your resort has a pool. Then enjoy a breakfast buffet or a quick sit-down meal. By mid-morning, check yourself out of the hotel (and give your bags to the bell person to hold if necessary). You are now free to explore. The boardwalk has many shops and attractions, and a beach. But don't run around too much; this is a vacation, after all! Have a late lunch and head home in the early to late afternoon.

Recommendations: The best activities for a cheap vacation are those which incur little or no cover charge. Shopping without buying is free, so take all the time at The Walk, The Quarter, or other shopping venues that suit your taste. At night, Trump Taj Mahal's Casbah club is sometimes cover charge-free. If you can afford a $16 taxi ride ($8 each way), then head over to Mixx at the Borgata, which sometimes has free cover. Buffets are expensive (frequently over $20 a person); so if you can, try cheaper counter service or the various fast-food options available in each resort.

Weekend with the Family
Vacation Time: *3 Days*
Best Time to Go: *Summertime*
Total Price: *$300 - $400 for 2 adults and 2 children*

Important Note: As stated before, family vacations can be very enjoyable in Atlantic City. However, the primary audience is adults. Therefore, children should be supervised at all times, and you must be aware that Atlantic City attracts primarily gamblers. Families with children of any age should avoid off-boardwalk property at night. Use good judgment in all cases.

That being said, a three day, two night vacation with children gives you the opportunity to go beyond the boardwalk and explore the rest of Atlantic City. You will need access to a car, because (1) access off-boardwalk requires driving, and (2) casino bus services require passengers to be 21 or over to receive the casino discount. Additionally, there are some very specific family attractions, not-to-be-missed, which are several miles off the boardwalk.

With a family, a summertime vacation is a must, and plan to stay at either Tropicana or Trump Taj Mahal, which are the most kid-friendly resorts in Atlantic City. While both offer coveted beach access, Tropicana has the magnificent new Quarter, which features an IMAX movie theater and numerous kitschy shopping venues. Trump Taj Mahal is the closest resort to Steel Pier, Atlantic City's amusement pier.

Arrive early in the afternoon to take advantage of daylight. Almost certainly the kids will want to explore Steel Pier first, so make that a priority on day one. The late hours of the pier mean that much time can be spent here; sometimes it is open until midnight. If you need a break from the rides, Ripley's Believe It or Not! museum is nearby, and can be a pleaser for teens (younger children may find some of the exhibits scary). Also, WOW! VR (a virtual reality simulator) is nearby.

For dinner, take the kids to a resort buffet (note: unfortunately, some buffets require patrons to be 21, such as the Virginia City Buffet). They are expensive but casual, and noisy kids running around may not be as much of a problem. At night, settle the kids in (if they are old enough) and have a quiet, romantic dinner or drink with your significant other.

On the morning of day two, take a swim if your resort has a pool, but don't get too tired out because Jersey Shore beach is a great place to spend the hottest afternoons. Breakfast can be had at your resort's 24-hour restaurant, but if you're still full from last night, you could get away with just that extra piece of fruit that you didn't eat from last night's buffet.

If the family is interested, Central Pier (just south of Steel Pier) is a smaller amusement pier, which features a nice go-cart track and some arcade games. The two other major arcades – Playcade Arcade and Atlantic City Boardwalk Arcade – offer a wider selection of games but without the go-cart track. These attractions are best suited for older children, mostly teens.

Storybook Land is a classic South Jersey Shore destination for very young children and their families. Definitely add this to your roster and plan on at least half a day for the experience. However, for kids of any age, Lucy the Elephant in Margate is a must. A short drive south, this attraction is one of the best in the Atlantic City area. It is small and quaint and won't use up much time (the tour through the six-story pachyderm is rarely longer than 30 minutes).

If there is time, and it is hot enough, an hour or two on the Jersey Shore beach is tough to beat! Stake out a nice spot near your resort, lay down a towel, put on your sunscreen, and get comfortable. The beach by Atlantic City is generally less crowded than the surrounding Jersey Shore beaches, such as Margate or Seaside.

In the late afternoon, head back to the boardwalk and check out Tropicana's The Quarter. The IMAX Theater here shows all kinds of movies, based on the current market. Houdini's Magic Shop has all sorts of whimsical items, and The Spy Store is just plain cool. With the kids at the movies, parents can enjoy the various clubs, comedy, or dining offered at Tropicana. Spending the evening here is the best way to wrap up day two.

Sleep in on the morning of day three. You probably don't need to check out of your room until 11:00 AM, so take advantage. After a nice breakfast, head over to The Walk, Atlantic City's outlet center. A unique indoor ride, Passport: Voyages of Discovery, is designed for younger children, but older children and teens may enjoy it as well. With the kids occupied for the better part of an hour (the attraction is rather long), you are free to do some serious shopping at the many outlet stores. When finished, grab a quick bite and head back home!

Beach and Backwoods Fun
Vacation Time: *2-3 Days*
Best Time to Go: *Summertime*
Total Price: *$100 - $200 for up to 2 people*

Atlantic City's close proximity to both beach and forest make it an ideal spot for people who like the outdoors, but don't want to leave the comforts of home far behind. To experience the best of outdoor activities, plan a summertime vacation.

Arrive in the early afternoon of day one. Before checking into to your hotel (you can opt for either an off-boardwalk or on-boardwalk resort, whichever you prefer), grab your beach towel and chair, and enjoy the hot summer sun! Jersey Shore water is surprisingly warm for a north Atlantic state.

Depending on how much you intend to do, you may decide to spend either one or two nights in the area. Relaxing on the beach is one thing, but tomorrow you will enjoy the thick wooded nature of New Jersey's largest state forest: Wharton.

On day two, load up your car and drive to nearby Wharton State Forest. Batsto Village serves as the central information area for activities in the forest, so if you're not sure what to do, head there first. Otherwise, you can hike, kayak (or canoe), horseback ride, or even camp if you have the time. The forest is large and in some places can get rather desolate.

On day three, or later in day two (depending on your schedule), jump from forested wilderness to coastal wetlands by visiting the Edwin B. Forsythe National Wildlife Refuge. Though mostly for birdwatching, the refuge provides a great long-distance view of the Atlantic City skyline, and an idea of what Absecon Island would look like undeveloped. The eight-plus-mile driving "safari" gives you some great panoramic views.

Recommendations: Even though summertime offers more activities, Batsto Village in Wharton State Forest is open year-round. There are many campgrounds, trails, and other outdoor activities throughout the forest and the rest of the Pine Barrens. The beach in Atlantic City is almost always less crowded than other places along the Jersey Shore. If you prefer more beach activity, consider going a few miles south on Absecon Island, to Margate or Longport (beach access sometimes incurs a fee in these neighboring communities, unlike Atlantic City, where access is always free). For daredevils, Lakes Bay offers some water sports. Extreme Windsurfing provides rental equipment and some training.

Romantic Retreat

Vacation Time: *3 Days*
Best Time to Go: *Crisp, chilly winter eves, when the crowds are sparse and the luxury suites are discounted*
Total Price: *$400 - $500 for 2 people*

Atlantic City is a very popular romantic destination. Spectacular ocean views, romantic restaurants, and lavish suites of every size and description make it a couple's paradise. Though most newlyweds may prefer a more exotic destination, honeymoons and wedding anniversaries are not uncommon here.

Since romantic getaways require a romantic room, a suite in one of the resorts is a must. Suites are abundant, but be warned: on weekends and holidays, suites are frequently reserved for high-profile gamblers. Therefore, you may either need to book well in advance, or consider booking on a weekday. Jacuzzi suites are popular; they are typically a regular-sized room with a Jacuzzi and shower instead of a bathtub. The highest-priced suites, with sizes sometimes exceeding 1,000 square feet, start at around $500 per night.

Recommendations: The nicest resort in Atlantic City is the Borgata. It is located off the boardwalk, but if you visit in wintertime and don't expect to do much resort-hopping, this setback might not matter. Though every resort has a romantic restaurant and bar, my favorite is in Tropicana, called Top of the Trop. For shopping, Historic Smithville is a peaceful place, with plenty of romantic spots, and even paddleboats on the small lake.

The Total Atlantic City Experience
Vacation Time: *4-5 Days*
Best Time to Go: *Summertime*
Total Price: *$600+ for 2-4 people*

If you want to experience much of Atlantic City, give yourself about three or four nights. That way, you can visit all the resorts, and many of the area's attractions, without giving yourself too much of a head spin.

Recommendations: follow the guidelines and descriptions in this book to plan the best vacation possible (of course, use other materials to plan your trip as well)!

One Final Note...

Atlantic City is in a time of wonderful change. New resorts, new attractions, and new ways to have fun are constantly being added. Old attractions are being refurbished and reinvented, faster than seems possible. We are indeed in the midst of something exciting.

The moment this book hits the press, chances are good that a new mega-attraction will surface, drawing mass media frenzy – just as the Borgata did in 2003. When that happens, this book will be a history lesson; a chapter in a halfway-completed saga of rebirth. I will be pleased when this book is out of date; for Atlantic City will have continued its growth and development.

Casino gambling was a start, but it has taken twenty-five years for Atlantic City to re-awaken from its slumber. This is a city that deserves the very best. And now, for the first time in decades, it is finally starting to come into its own.

Atlantic City is on its way.

INTERNET DIRECTORY

The Internet is a vast pool of knowledge. Unfortunately, however, most of it is pure garbage (type "Atlantic City" into any web search engine and you'll see what I mean). But there are a few diamonds in the rough. Since I believe strongly in the power of Internet research, and since you are recommended to research on your own prior to committing to a vacation, I have taken care to list some of the better Atlantic City web sites below, in addition to the web sites referenced throughout the rest of this book.

All of these sites have been browsed and utilized by myself. Please note that I am not officially endorsing any of these sites. I am providing this information because I have found these sights helpful in planning my trips to Atlantic City, and as research in compiling information for this book.

Atlantic City Boardwalk Hall
http://www.boardwalkhall.com

This site provides information on the history of the Boardwalk Hall, as well as the schedule of both ongoing and one-time events. It offers fairly in-depth information, and is good for browsing.

Atlantic City Convention & Visitor's Authority
http://www.atlanticcitynj.com

This is the official website for the Atlantic City Visitor's Authority and is geared towards tourism. It is extremely comprehensive; it lists much of what there is to do in and around Atlantic City (including some of the surrounding area). It offers extensive hotel and attraction listings, operating hours, and newsworthy items. A first-time or returning visitor to Atlantic City might benefit greatly from visiting this site.

Atlantic City Historical Museum
http://www.acmuseum.net

The Atlantic City Historical Museum's website has information about the museum on Garden Pier, as well as some basic historical facts on the area's elaborate history.

Atlantic City Outlets – "The Walk"
http://www.acoutlets.com

This is the official site for the Atlantic City outlet mall located across from Caesars and Bally's. It describes the place, as well as operating hours and stores which are currently open or coming soon.

Atlantic City Reservations
http://www.atlanticcity.com

Although it's generally advised for you to book your stay directly with the hotel of your choice, this method might not always be the best option. If you don't care what hotel you stay at, you could use a large commercial travel agency (such as Travelocity or Expedia – both very fine agencies) but they probably will not have the best room rates or availability information for the big resort-hotels. However, this website does! There are several sites that focus on just reservations for Atlantic City, and they all appear to use the same basic engine utilized by this site, which is much more focused on Atlantic City than a larger, more commercial agency.

Atlantic City Surf / Sandcastle Stadium
http://www.acsurf.com

Comprehensive website on the Atlantic City Surf baseball team as well as their home, Sandcastle Stadium. There are links to other baseball-related sights, and you can buy tickets online.

Atlantic City Hilton Hotel and Casino
http://www.caesars.com/Hilton/atlanticcity/

This is the official website for the Atlantic City Hilton. It is part of the Caesars Entertainment website. It functions similarly to the websites for Bally's Park Place and Caesars Atlantic City. This is the best place to book online for hotel reservations. There is also a "special offers" section that allows you to see a calendar and how much rooms would cost on any given date (this is a very useful feature to see hotel prices at a glance). You can also track your casino comp dollars if you are a gambler. You cannot book suites on this site, however, and there is no indication that suites even exist. For that, you'd have to call the hotel directly. There is also restaurant/bar, casino, and show information available on this site.

Atlantic City Miniature Golf
http://www.acminigolf.com

This small website will give you a general idea of what Atlantic City Miniature Golf is all about, including operating hours and other pieces of important information.

Balic Winery
http://www.balicwinery.com

Site devoted to Balic Winery. It contains information on the different types of wine that the vineyard produces, as well as some information on visiting.

Bally's Atlantic City / Bally's Park Place
http://www.ballysac.com

This is the official website for Bally's Atlantic City. It is part of the Caesars Entertainment website. It functions similarly to the websites for the Atlantic City Hilton and Caesars Atlantic City. This is the best place to book online for hotel reservations. There is also a "special offers" section that allows you to see a calendar and how much rooms would cost on any given date (this is a very useful to see hotel prices at a glance). If you gamble you can also track your casino comp dollars. Although the best suites require you to call and make a reservation, you can still book some of the lower-level suites online (such as a Jacuzzi suite). When you book a room with Bally's you may get either a room in the regular Bally's Tower or in their Claridge Casino tower. There is also information on this site about Bally's Wild Wild West Casino, including types of games available, and restaurant/bar information.

Borgata Hotel Casino & Spa
http://www.theborgata.com

This is my favorite of all the Atlantic City resort-hotel websites. It is very well-designed and Flash-y (both kinds of "Flash"-y! Web designers... forgive my stupid joke). You can book rooms online and even book their lower-level suites online, get spa or show information or, if a gambler, check your casino comp balance. A lot of thought was obviously put into the marketing of the Borgata. Building a new resort-hotel in Atlantic City after thirteen years was really a "gamble."

Caesars Atlantic City
http://www.caesarsac.com

This is the official website for Caesars Atlantic City. It is part of the Caesars Entertainment website. It functions similarly to the websites for Bally's Park Place and the Atlantic City Hilton. This is the best place to book online for hotel reservations. There is also a "special offers" section that allows you to see a calendar and how much rooms would cost on any given date (this is a very useful feature to see hotel prices at a glance). You can also track your casino comp dollars. You cannot book suites on this site, however, and there is no indication that suites even exist. For that, you'd have to call the hotel directly. There is also restaurant/bar, casino, and show information available on this site.

Chicken Bone Beach
http://www.chickenbonebeach.org

This is the official website for the Chicken Bone Beach Historical Foundation, Inc. It provides historical insight as well as information about their annual summertime concert series in Kennedy Plaza.

Club Tru
http://www.clubtru.com

Official website for one of Atlantic City's largest and most well known nightspots. This site features information about the various activities available, special event listings, and an extensive collection of photographs from various club events.

Flyers Skate Zone
http://www.flyersskatezone.com

Devoted to the Philadelphia Flyers Skate Zone chain of ice rinks, including the one in Atlantic City. Site also features links to various hockey-related information.

Hamilton Mall
http://www.shophamilton.com

This is the official mall website. It has a comprehensive directory of stores and phone numbers, as well as operating hours and listings of mall special events (if any). It also advertises for some of the shops, with various offers.

Harrah's Atlantic City
Harrah's Showboat
http://www.harrahs.com

Information on all of Harrah's resort-hotels can be found at one single location. Here you can find general information about each location, as well as book rooms online. Each resort does not have its own website. I wonder if this will change, now that Harrah's has acquired Caesars Entertainment.

Lucy the Elephant
http://www.lucytheelephant.com

You can find out about some of Lucy's history, learn how to get to the attraction, including operating hours, and even buy Lucy souvenirs online.

Marine Mammal Stranding Center
http://www.mmsc.org

Official website for the center; includes lots of useful information on tours, operating schedules, and the general operating procedures.

Miss America
http://www.missamerica.org

This is the official site for the Miss America Organization. It is completely thorough, with lots of information about the scholarship competitions and pageants. It goes in-depth into the history of the organization, including a list of every Miss America winner, as well as extensive biographies and photos and lists of upcoming events and shows.

Ocean Life Center
http://www.oceanlifecenter.com

This site features information on the Ocean Life Center in Gardner's Basin, including directions and operating house. Also includes brief descriptions of their main exhibits and attractions. Features a floor plan of the facility.

Passport: Voyages of Discovery
http://www.passportvoyages.com

This highly intensive Flash website tells you about the various locations for this attraction, and gives you some company information. Be warned: you need a fast internet connection, as this site will gobble up your bandwidth!

Renault Winery
http://www.renaultwinery.com

Comprehensive website covering the entire Renault resort complex. Here you can inquire about the vineyard tour, Tuscany House, the on-property restaurants, golf course information, and some history on the area.

Resorts Atlantic City
http://www.resortsac.com

You can book your Resorts reservation online at this website, including a limited number of suites and Jacuzzi rooms, and you can find out about the different types of attractions available on-site. The site makes it clear that complimentary rooms cannot be booked online. This is true with most resorts in the area – most complimentary rooms must be booked through casino services.

Ripley's *Believe It or Not!*
http://www.ripleys.com

This is the official website for Ripley's Entertainment. This includes all Ripley's *Believe It or Not!* locations, as well as locations for Ripley's Moving Theater, Ripley's Aquarium, and Ripley's Haunted Adventure (most of these attractions are not in Atlantic City).

Sands Casino Hotel
http://www.sandsac.com

Here you can get all the information you need about the Sands. You can book online for both the Sands and the nearby Madison House Tower (a separate hotel but under the same corporate blanket). Again, however, there are no indications of suites as far as I can tell – but there is a calendar feature that shows room rates at a glance (similar to the Caesars sites).

Steel Pier
http://www.steelpier.com

This is the official Steel Pier site. Here you can get a very basic idea of the kinds of attractions available in the park, as well as prices and operating hours.

Storybook Land
http://www.storybookland.com

Main website for the Storybook Land children's amusement park. Includes an operating calendar with special events noted, as well as a general description of the park, and driving directions.

Tropicana
http://www.tropicana.net

One of the easier-to-navigate and friendlier Atlantic City hotel websites, here you can book reservations for rooms and some suites online. You can also find out lots of cool information about the resort. (Unless you want to learn about orange juice, be sure to access ".net" and not ".com".)

Trump Marina
http://www.trumpmarina.com

This is an adorable and well-designed website (very cartoonish yet classy). However, like all Trump websites for Atlantic City, you cannot book your room reservation online – you have to call them directly for the latest availability and quotes.

Trump Plaza
http://trumpplaza.com

This website describes for you all the different attractions available at Trump Plaza, but as with the other Trump hotels in Atlantic City, does not allow you to make a room reservation online. It only prompts you to call the hotel directly. Booking Trump hotel rooms is not an easy task (if possible at all) to do online.

Trump Taj Mahal
http://www.trumptaj.com

This website describes for you all the different attractions available at the Trump Taj Mahal, including rates for various rooms. It even describes the types of suites that are available. However, as of this writing, the site does not allow you to book any room reservations. It only prompts you to call the hotel directly. In fact, it is difficult to find any online site that will allow you to book rooms directly for this resort.

MORE INFORMATION

The following sources will provide additional information to help you better plan your next Atlantic City vacation, and perhaps to visit more of the famous Jersey Shore!

Africano, Lillian and Africano, Nina. Insiders' Guide to the Jersey Shore. Published by Globe Pequot. 1st Edition, 2002. 360 Pages.

Edelstein, Jeff. The Best of Everything at the Jersey Shore. Published by New Jersey Monthly Press. 1st Edition 1999. 111 Pages.

Futrell, Jim. Amusement Parks of New Jersey. Published by Stackpole Books. 2004. 227 Pages.

Levi, Vicki Gold and Eisenberg, Lee. Atlantic City: 125 Years of Ocean Madness. Published by Ten Speed Press. 2nd Edition, 1994. 214 Pages.

Roberts, Russell and Youmans, Rich. Down the Jersey Shore. Published by Rutgers University Press, 1993. 290 Pages.

Santelli, Robert. Guide to the Jersey Shore. Published by Globe Pequot. 6th Edition, 2003. 240 Pages.

INDEX

A

Absecon Lighthouse, 26, 35, 110, 152, 153
Adrian Phillips Ballroom, 64, 140
Amphora Lounge, 121
Andrew Geller, 70
Animations Coffee Shop, 84
Asian Spice, 99
Atlantic City Art Center, 149, 185
Atlantic City Bar & Grill, 198
Atlantic City Country Club, 145
Atlantic City Hilton, 43, 51, 52, 53, 54, 67, 89, 103, 145, 154, 213, 214
Atlantic City Historical Museum, 148, 185, 212
Atlantic City Miniature Golf, 134, 185, 213
Atlantic City Outlets, 76, 169, 212
Atlantus Charters, 167
Aztar, 55

B

B. Gentlemen, 104
Babalu Grill, 198
Bacchanal, 72
Back Bay Ale House, 166
Back Bay Ice Cream, 166
Bagel & Doughnut Connection, 90
Balic Winery, 157, 213
Bare Exposure, 180
Bath Junkie, 104
Batsto Village, 162, 163, 164, 207, 208
Bayside Buffet, 126
B-Bar, 120
Beach Ball Deli and Seafood House, 99
Beach Bar, 63, 64, 71, 110
Beachfront Buffet, 58
Bel Haven Canoes and Kayaks, 164
Bellezza, 53, 70
Bernie Robbins, 104, 127
Best Western Atlantic City West Extended Stay & Suites, 195
Best Western Envoy Inn, 192
Best Western Garden State Inn, 194
Big Easy Spa, 108
Bikini Beach Bar, 84
Blue Heron Pines Golf Club, 144
Blue Martini, 84, 85
Bluepoint, 115
Boardwalk Buffet, 95
Boardwalk Favorites, 58
Boardwalk Hall, 29, 37, 61, 85, 133, 139, 140, 141, 142, 185, 190, 211
Boardwalk Peanut Shoppe, 110, 127
Boardwalk Treats, 104
Boardwalker Bar, 63
Bombay Café, 103
Borgata Comedy Club, 121
Borgata Hotel Casino & Spa, 214
Brandeis Jewelers, 70
Breadsticks Café & Grill, 99

Brighton Steakhouse, 94
Broadway Buffet, 63
Brooks Brothers, 59

C

Cache, 64
Camelot, 99
Canal Street Bread and Sandwich
    Co., 110
Capriccio, 99
Caprice, 99
Casa Di Napoli, 109
Casbah, 104, 122, 127, 177, 205
Casbah Café, 104
Central Pier Arcade & Speedway,
    133, 185
Chelsea Cafe, 199
China Café, 63
Circus Maximus Theatre, 70, 72
Civil Rights Garden, 149, 150
Claridge Casino Hotel, 86
Claridge Gift Shop, 90
Clarion Hotel Convention Center
    Atlantic City, 195
Club Cappuccino, 115
Club Tru, 178, 179, 215
Coconutz, 180
Colonial Inn, 174
Comedy Stop at Tropicana, 57
Comfort Inn Atlantic City, 191
Comfort Inn North, 193
Comfort Inn Victorian, 195
Comfort Inn West, 195
Copa Lounge, 95
Copa Room, 95
Corner, 95, 115
Corner Express, 95
Corner Grille, 115
Cuba Libre, 59

D

David Charles Salon, 114
Days Inn Absecon, 193
Days Inn Atlantic City, 191
Dino Roberts, 127
Dizzy Dolphin, 53
Docksider, 128
Donald Trump, 61, 97, 101
Dr. Jonathon Pitney House, 151,
    152, 193
Dynasty, 102

E

Econo Lodge Absecon, 193
Econo Lodge Beach Block, 191
Econo Lodge Boardwalk, 192
Edwin B. Forsythe National
    Wildlife Refuge, 30, 162, 163,
    208
El Greco Motel, 191
Emporium, 53
Empress Breakfast Buffet, 52
Empress Garden, 52
Erwin Pearl, 59
Event Center, 121
EVO, 63
Exclusively Taj, 104
Extreme Windsurfing, 167, 208

F

Fairfield Inn Absecon, 193
Fantasea Reef Buffet, 115
Farley State Marina, 125, 127,
    128, 156
Firewaters, 58
Fitness Center, 114
Flying Cloud Cafe, 199
Fortunes, 63
French Quarter Buffet, 109
Front Page Gift Shop, 64

Fulu Noodle Bar, 91

G

Garden Café, 90
Gladiator Grille, 72
Gold Tooth Gerties Buns & Bagels, 79
Golden Dynasty, 57
Golf Courses, 144
Grand Cayman, 126, 127
Grill, 84, 95
Gypsy Bar, 120

H

Hamilton Mall, 175, 215
Hampton Inn Atlantic City Absecon, 194
Harbor Pines Golf Club, 145
Harbor View, 126
Hard Rock Café, 18, 103
Harley-Davidson Store, 104
High Roller, 167
High Steaks, 126
Hilton Beach Bar, 53
Historic Smithville, 173, 174, 175, 209
Holiday Inn Boardwalk, 191
Holiday Inn Express Absecon, 194
Holiday Inn Express Atlantic City, 195
Hooters, 58, 126
Horizons, 53
Howard Johnson Downtown, 192
Howard Johnson Express Inn Absecon, 194
Howard Johnson Hotel Atlantic City, 191
Hunan Chinese Restaurant, 199

I

Icahn, 93
IMAX, 59, 205, 206
Imperial Court, 126
Imperial Inn, 199
Irish Pub & Inn, 199
Island BBQ Buffet, 53

J

Johnny Rockets, 84

K

Knife & Fork Inn, 200
Korean War Memorial, 26, 87, 149, 185

L

La Piazza, 72
Landau Jewelers, 70
Le Salon, 53
Living Room, 119, 120
Lobby Lounge, 84
Lobster Shanty, 166
Lone Star Snack Bar, 79
Los Amigos, 200
Lucy the Elephant, 153, 154, 194, 206, 216
Luna, 84

M

Mansion Café, 110
MarketPlace, 56, 57, 58
Medici, 94
Miss America Organization, 141, 216
Mixx, 120, 121, 122, 177, 205
Moon, 102, 156
Mountain Bar, 78, 79, 85
Music Box, 121

N

N.O.W., 121
New Yorker, 63
Noodle Bar, 109
Noodles & Zen Sum, 84
Noyes Museum, 159

O

Oaks Steakhouse, 52
Oasis, 103
Ocean 11 Gift Shop, 110
Ocean Life Center, 26, 156, 165, 166, 216
Ombra, 120, 121
Opa, 171, 200

P

Palladium Ballroom, 70
Party Pit, 70, 73
Passport: Voyages of Discovery, 135, 136, 207, 217
Peanut Shoppe, 95
Perfect 10 Martini Lounge, 179
Planet Hollywood, 18, 73, 103
Playcade Arcade, 133, 185, 206
Playground, 148, 180
Plaza Spa, 64
Portofino, 126
Primavera, 72
Prime Place, 82, 84
prostitution, 181

Q

Quality Inn and Suites, 193
Quality Inn Beach Block, 192
Quality Inn Pleasantville, 195
Quarter, 56, 57, 58, 59, 71, 108, 109, 110, 205, 206

R

Rainforest Café, 63
Ramada Limited, 195
Reflections Café, 115
Renault Gourmet Restaurant, 158
Renault Winery, 145, 157, 159, 217
Resorts Atlantic City, 97, 98, 217
Resorts Gifts and News, 99
Retail Piazza, 120
Rib & Chophouse, 109
Risi Bisi, 121
Rodeway Inn, 191, 192, 193
Rodeway Inn Absecon, 193
Rodeway Inn Atlantic City, 191

S

Sand Box Beach Bar, 71
Sandcastle Baseball Stadium, 143
Sbarro, 103
Scheherazade, 103
Screening Room, 99
Seaview Resort and Spa, 145
Sheraton Atlantic City, 191
Shore Bet Fishing, 167
Shore Mall, 173
Showboat Atlantic City, 107, 110
Sidewalk Café, 84
Siganos Plaza, 170, 171
Skate Zone, 143, 144, 194, 215
Smithville Inn, 173, 174
Sound of Philadelphia, 59
Spa and Gardens, 122
Spa at Caesars, 70
Spa Café, 85
Spa Pro Shop, 85
Speccio, 120, 121
Special Effects, 99
Spy Store, 59, 207
Stage Deli of New York, 103
Starbucks, 63, 95, 110, 170

Steakhouse, 63, 115
Steel Pier, 24, 29, 36, 104, 131, 132, 134, 185, 205, 206, 218
Storybook Land, 137, 138, 206, 218
Strip Clubs, 179
Studio Six, 179
Super 8 Atlantic City, 192
Superstar Theater, 99
Surfside Resort Hotel, 179
Swingers, 95

T

Talk of the Walk, 99, 114, 127
Teen Center, 115
Temple Bar, 68, 72
The Arena, 104
The Buffet, 99
The Deck, 126, 127
The Shell, 127
The Wave, 127, 177
Theater at the Hilton, 53
Tiffany Lounge, 57
Top of the Trop, 57, 209
Travelodge Atlantic City Absecon, 193
Tropicana, 55, 56, 57, 58, 59, 71, 72, 98, 126, 133, 139, 190, 191, 204, 205, 206, 209, 218
Tropicana Showroom, 57
Tru Energy Bar, 179

Trump Marina, 111, 125, 126, 127, 128, 156, 165, 177, 218
Trump Plaza, 61, 62, 63, 64, 65, 139, 180, 219
Trump Taj Mahal, 98, 101, 102, 103, 104, 105, 109, 127, 131, 132, 150, 171, 177, 192, 204, 205, 219
Tun Tavern, 200
Tuscany House, 158, 217
Twenties Steakhouse, 90
Twisted Dune Golf Club, 144

U

Upstairs Café, 126

V

Verdi, 57
Vineyard Golf, 158
Virginia City Buffet, 79, 80

W

Wharton State Forest, 30, 162, 163, 164, 196, 207, 208
White House Sub Shop, 201
Wok & Roll, 91
Wonder Bar, 201

X

Xanadu, 104

ABOUT THE AUTHOR

Born and raised in Chicago, Dirk Vander Wilt has academic degrees in film and television production and music composition from New York University. He is a consumate traveler and authority on "tack", be it quality or otherwise.

Printed in the United States
42768LVS00002B/276